AF414919

Table of Contents

PRISONS: THE LOCKDOWN OF BLACK (AMERICA'S FUTURE)

There is no doubt that the *overwhelming majority of white Americans desire that there be as few Negroes as possible in America.* If the Negroes could be eliminated from America or greatly decreased in numbers, this would meet the whites' approval – provided that it could be accomplished by means which are also approved...

In our further discussion of the means in Negro population policy, we ought start out from the desire of the politically dominant white population to get rid of the Negroes. This is a goal difficult to reach by approved means, and the desire has never been translated into action directly, and probably never will be. All the most obvious means go strongly against the American Creed...

Gunnar Myrdal writing in: An American Dilemma:
The Negro Problem and Modern Democracy, 1944

PREFACE TO THE 2020 EDITION

PRISONS: The Lockdown of Black (America's Future) was initially published in 1996. It was the seventh in a series of *Conscious Rasta Reports* that were completed in that year. It was originally intended that the Reports would be bi-monthly research journals. That first year was so productive because I was able to draw upon many shorter topical reports, which I could gather several together and publish in a larger book form.

By the end of 1999, I was able to complete 18 books in this series. The appearance of **PRISONS** signaled a milestone for me. From that point onward, each new report was begun from scratch; a single unifying theme sets the tone for the whole publication. As I set upon this heightened pathway, the research became much more focused and in-depth. As such, the rate at which I would be able to complete and publish each new book slowed. In 1997, I was able to complete four further editions.

The series of Reports culminated with the end of the decade witnessing the birth of my tour-de-force **THE ROAD TO POWER: *Seven Steps to an African Global Order***. That book also signaled another change in the format in which I published each new book. Rather than use a standard research report book size as was the bulk of the series, I then moved to print in the standard book form that fit in shelves just like the rest of my library.

This edition of **PRISONS** is being republished to satisfy several needs. First, my third print run of the original format has been depleted and needed to be replenished in my inventory. Second, the entirety of the catalog of *Conscious Rasta Reports* is a significant contribution to research literature from a distinctly African-centered perspective. I am convinced that the entire body of these 18 Reports could serve as a robust curriculum for the advance of a new style of highly-functioning leadership. The masthead, which has appeared on all of these Reports, reads: *Cutting Edge Research to Serve An Emerging Leadership.*   As such, this edition is a much-needed contribution for those leaders who need to have more in-depth research, insight, and precise data on the phenomenon of incarceration in the U.S.

Third, there needed to be an up-to-date data source that could serve professionals in the criminal justice system. I could never have imagined just how impactful would be this book as I struggled to get it completed, published, printed, and distributed.

I determined that the content within this book would be highly valuable to individuals caught within the system, along with their families. As such, I decided to upload the entire book to the Internet for the benefit of anyone who wanted to access it at no cost. In 1996, the worldwide web was still a radical new transformation for information access and exchange.

Because of my 5-year affiliation with the Washington D.C. based think tank, **The Information Project For Africa (IPFA)**, I was one of the very first of the African-centered community to have my work published on the Internet. To this date, I still have heard people report that my work was the first such culturally centered work they had seen on the web. I will admit that my invitation to become a member of this international journalists' collective was a significant breakthrough in my science, research, and publishing career.

After pushing this entire book up on the Internet, a few exciting events entered my attention, leading me to later fully comprehend the impact of my writing on the larger society.

As the Internet was so radically new, and search engines were something that produced a surprising, almost fantastic outcome, I would periodically type my name into a search engine and see what results would come up. Shortly after publishing **PRISONS** as a freely available eBook download, I noticed that it appeared on a wide variety of online sources. It certainly had much larger acknowledgment than any of the other published writings in my catalog. To my surprise, the most frequent links to the book were posted by law enforcement agencies, an outcome which hadn't been at the forefront of my imagination when I committed to freely sharing the book.

I immediately came to understand how the book was popular with law enforcement agencies; the data included in **PRISONS** was quite comprehensive and up to date. As such, criminal justice professionals were using my book to bolster their research and criminal law policies. While this did allow me a measure of gratification that my research was being taken seriously by these professionals, it had always been my intent that this book would help to *alleviate* the great harm and devastation that rapidly-increasing incarceration was causing to families, communities, and the larger society.

Another surprise was that I began receiving invitations from the U.S. Department of Justice to apply for federally-supported research grants. What a surprise!

Years earlier, I had twice applied for grants under the Public Corporation for the Arts (PCA). Twice applied, twice denied. The second denial even saw someone that I knew and trusted get a $2500 PCA grant *using my very idea* as his proposal. Not only did he get the award after copying my concept, he subsequently asked me to help him to complete the project for which he would get paid. I turned him down and quickly soured on the process of applying for grants. I was entirely burned on the process of begging the federal government to support my artistic, creative, and investigative talents; I committed to getting things done on my terms.

So, it was an unwelcome surprise to receive a grant proposal for $2500 from the Department of Justice (DOJ) to produce research for them. I threw their solicitation in the trash right away. Over the next several years, I received more Solicitations for Research with accompanying grant opportunities.

As I am writing in 2020, I just fished through bookshelves for 10 minutes. I found several of these solicitations from the U.S. Department of Justice National Institute of Justice, along with more recently published examples of the research that they were seeking:

• Solicitation for Research and Evaluation on Violence Against Women: Fiscal Year 1996

• Solicitation for Policing Research and Evaluation: Fiscal Year 1996

• Office of Juvenile Justice and Delinquency Prevention (OJJDP): Matrix of Community-Based Initiatives

• A second program from OJJDP: Juvenile Offenders and Victims: 1996 Update on Violence

These are only part of multiple solicitations from the federal government which were mailed to me referring to my *nom de plum* (my writing moniker) and not addressed to the taxpayer name by which the federal government usually would be contacting me. This led me to conclude that it was the publication of **PRISONS** that brought me to their attention – at least outwardly so.

I kept tossing these grant solicitations in the trash, although I did note that with each subsequent request, the grant offerings kept doubling. When these solicitations reached as high as $60,000 and later $120,000 annual research grants, I stopped throwing them into the trash. Somewhere, buried in 23 years of accumulated papers in my library, I still have details of those requests.

I needed the money. Back in the late 1990s, this was a lot of money.   Calculating the value of $60,000 in 1997, it would today be the equivalent of nearly $96,000. Not responding to a research grant offer of $120,000 for a year's worth of work, I would, in today's dollars, be turning down over $191,000. What in the hell was I thinking about?

Today, I would probably take the money. I needed it badly then. I was married had three children ranging in age from three to eight years. My income from the music industry was downshifting to that of an author of books for Blacks; another way of saying that I was steadily going bankrupt. If anyone needed such a cash windfall, I was indeed a candidate.

Still, I held out for purely ideological reasons -- well, almost strictly ideological. There was the consideration that if I did take the money for one year, could I create a cash flow to keep up with my new level of expenses so that, for the next year, I might not have to rely upon the DOJ to issue me more grants. I knew of some of these African American perpetual grant employees, and I didn't have a tremendous amount of respect for that process.

Over the years that have followed, fiscally, I've suffered immensely, the details of which I will spare the reader. The quality of my research has continued to rise to higher standards for accuracy and depth. My ability to use scientific futurism to gain macro vision over a broad landscape of relevance and possibilities has risen to truly global heights. The price I paid in not becoming a grant employee of the U.S. Department of Justice has led me to a considerable measure of self-respect that compliments my whole life.

Several people have long been aware of these types of stories that have experienced over the past 40 years of cultural and political advocacy. Such dear friends have accompanied me across a journey that has carried us deep into respect, fellowship, and committed collaboration.   For these relationships and the integrity upon which they have been built, I am much compensated. I would even go so far as to say that the Most High Creator has an appreciation for those who don't take a less risky pathway only to compromise a part of their essential integrity for money compensation.

I know of and have met no small number of people who live within such compromise, renting a piece of their soul for a reliable paycheck. Too often, these are not happy people. Some live to work toward retirement. Upon such retirement, too often, they are so unhappy that their health begins to decline immediately. I do not plan to go out like that.

This brings me to today, and this effort to update, error-check, and republish **PRISONS**. As I am reading it through again for the umpteenth time, I do see that it was very significant work. The data in it was spot on and way ahead of what the public was receiving from mainstream media. Mine was a competent mind exploring a phenomenon which had not yet gripped the national attention, yet eventually became a significant drain on national resources, community, and family life.

Much of my work from 1991 was centered upon themes of racial injustice, eugenics, population control, and social engineering. During the years that have followed, I observed the nation's three-decades-long incarceration surge in these terms.   It is often said that hindsight is indispensable. As I watch these changes over the decades since the first publication of **PRISONS**, it is evident that my original suspicions were not only correct but profoundly futurist in a fundamental way.

I had intended that there would be a widespread response, reaction, action, and strategic organizing to derail this process that has led to the jailing of millions of vulnerable people during this time that has passed. For Blacks in America, this orgy of incarceration has proven particularly harmful. The disruption has affected individual lives, young couples, and the families which they were raising, extended families, communities, municipalities, as well as states, regions, and the nation at large.

In many ways, this book reads like a time capsule. We cannot go back and recover the damage to so many lives over these past decades. If we are wise, we can learn from the past to engage our contemporary, to avert a future of further disruption to social order and evolution of our communities.

In no small way, I have become more pessimistic about the next three to four decades ahead. Working these insights from the position of *scientific futurism,* I have come to a troubling projection about the next forty-five years regarding the future for African Americans – I don't see this group as capable of overcoming the debilitating trends that have seized the fate of our ethnicity.

As you examine the details of this book, see these trends with the luxury of over 25 years of hindsight, you may come to the same conclusions as I have. We, as a group, were not able to use this widely-available information to transform our destiny, and have since born e witness to a significant injury to our people on a vast scale.   Subsequently, the many books that I have published since 1996 that put the spotlight on other damages to our people will be likely ignored as well.

We just don't seem to have respect for our own brilliance; this is particularly true concerning scientific futurism.

The old riddle asks of the ancient black population that inhabited western Asia long before Persia, Mesopotamia, and Babylon, "What happened to the people of Sumer?" The tragic answer is: "They disappeared because they forgot their history."

What will become the fate of Africans in America over the next half-century?   We have forgotten our history.   We have sacrificed the imperative to form families and raise healthy enough, prepared children to support continued existence and to thrive within our communities.

We don't produce enough food, shelter, industry, and thriving businesses to supply but 14 percent of our consumption. We thus trade our labor for survival at a rate that could be best calculated at 70 cents on the dollar.

Our group has lost 85% of its land acreage in the last century as our population tripled. Now our urban communities are being gentrified at an ever-faster pace, with huge populations being shifted from this nation's core economic centers toward suburban *bantustans* where there is very little industrial employment and insufficient number s and qualities of service jobs to sustain ourselves.

We cannot be allowed to forget our history if we are to survive. Many great nations have fallen from their civilization power throughout millennia of world history; ours certainly would not be the first to do so. It seems at times that we are acting as if we are deliberately committing *race suicide*.

We cannot be allowed to forget this history of **PRISONS: The Lockdown of Black, America's Future**.

Chapter 1 – INTRODUCTION

This report was initiated in 1994 as part of an extended set of reports I called *The Police State: Amerikkka 1995*. That group of publications detailed various aspects of the development of the sciences of population control . It included reports on police and military technology, changes in law enforcement, the judiciary, juvenile incarceration, along with other aspects of what I perceived were developments toward the wholesale restriction of specified targeted communities. I linked it all to social engineering resulting from national security policies, which were part of an evolving *fascist* ideology within American politics.

The original title of this report, when released in October 1994, was *Amerikkka: The World's Biggest Prison*, and as that title indicated, by that time this country had achieved the dubious record of the highest number of jailed citizens of any country on the planet, even more than such (similarly) oppressive nations like South Africa, Russia, and China.

Today, some two years later, the trends toward incarceration have continued to swing further toward oppression. The rate of jailing is particularly bitter for the *so-called* minorities within America, in particular those of African, Puerto Rican, and Latin American descent. While the main focus of this report will be on the relationship between Africans and the American prison system, much of the enclosed text will be equally as relevant to the other non-white ethnic groups, those Spanish speaking members and certain Pacific Islanders residing in the U.S.

While not wishing to trivialize or discriminate against other people of color, it is such a broad scope already examining the prison/incarceration system in the context of its effect on the Black community, and no one could deny that Blacks in America have disproportionately felt the sting of the incarceration system.

In this report, I wish to illuminate such topics as:

•The phenomenal increase in incarceration rates since the so-called civil rights movement,

•The gross disproportion of Africans in the system,

•Trends in juvenile imprisonment,

•Women in prison,

•Jailhouse lifestyle,

•The exploitation of cheap prison labor,

•"Cruel and unusual punishment,"

•The role of drugs in the rapid expansion of prison populations,

•The development of a prison-construction economic windfall,

•Pointing out social trends (such as poverty, miseducation, electronic media, and racism), which exacerbate the crisis,

•State-sanctioned execution,

•Perhaps most important, the larger impact of generations of young people being removed from their duty as producers and defenders of their particular community.

This is, without a doubt, a daunting analysis. The necessity of providing such an analysis is obvious – anything that might help Black people to derail this train that is carrying our future into a new form of enslavement is of immeasurable value. In the past, I have become aware that various of my *Conscious Rasta Reports* have been instrumental in changing people's reality and even helping large groups of people to define their agenda and to *buck the system*. That is the purpose of the Report.

Today between 56 and 68 million persons of African descent in America stand on the precipice of a future in which we will largely be irrelevant in domestic affairs, grossly impoverished, rigidly managed as a collective group, propagandized against as the scourge of the planet and jailed at the highest rate of any ethnic group in the industrialized world.

The net sum of all this negative development over the coming decades is that we stand to lose our place in the family of humanity and, because of deliberate policies of those managers of an American police state, the U.S. national security establishment, we are in actual danger of wholesale genocide and extinction.

I hope that this report will be of value to the political leaders, community activists, anti-incarceration organizers, to those who find themselves locked in the belly of the beast, to youth at risk, to family members of prisoners as well as to anyone who has the concern that this extreme targeting of ethnic groups for imprisonment is deleterious to a people's future. This is life-changing research, and somehow, somewhere in this larger text, all of these groups should find some enlightenment in this research report.

According to my dire predictions, this trend toward wholesale incarceration of Blacks, Hispanics, poor Whites, and other *undesired populations within America* will not only continue but worsen in the foreseeable future, this despite the apparent trend of declining rates of serious crime. I will attempt to illustrate that this is a deliberate and preconceived outcome, even though the implications of demonstrating that *conspiracy* goes far beyond this one report. Those familiar with the *Conscious Rasta Report* are aware that I have linked these ethnic and racial policies to the larger agenda of population control in an increasingly crowded (and non-white) global reality.

Thus I view the wholesale jailing of a significant proportion of the reproductive-age youth of specific communities as instrumental in eventually lowering the rate of childbirth within that targeted community. In essence, what I am proposing is that we begin to look at the tendency to incarcerate large numbers of a population group as a demented form of birth control.

Until Black leaders, as well as those who lead other ethnic groups, begin to view this wholesale imprisonment as a form of population control and social engineering, I am convinced that they will continue to promote irrelevant proposals and political movements or, worse yet, advocate policies which are contrary to the best interests of their constituency.

As always, I don't think that the mere submission to supernatural forces, promotion of "American values," handwringing or finger-pointing at invisible forces is going to do much if anything to resolve our short-term and long-term dilemmas. I believe that it is accurate research and analysis combined with effective policies of that political and social leadership, along with sufficient commitment of public resources that will change our reality. My contribution to that effort is the production to *accurate research and analysis* and thus, without the commitment of the other aspects of this effort to change our reality, this report will provide little or nothing toward the resolution of our incarceration crisis.

In the past, I have not only been called upon as a concerned individual to provide this analysis but to become a leader, worker, financier, and manager of the solution. Experience has shown that this is a mistake to make a dedicated member of the academic community take upon so many difficult tasks and is indicative that failure is imminent. In the future, if I or any other analyst produces research of profound value, and we are not backed up by the larger community, then we are doomed to failure in the short term.   The profound value of this point cannot be understated.   This is the way that it works in the larger community within America; that segment of the population that is empowered, enriched, accomplishes most of its goals and operates out of their own will and not the manipulation of an elite minority.

Barring no interruption of the trends which have become evident, within the coming decades Africans in America will suffer the undue loss of community resources because so many of our youth and productive age population have been shackled, imprisoned and shunted away to the fringe of society because of America's phenomenal rate of incarceration.   This process must be interrupted before Blacks can reclaim a sense of destiny and begin to raise the status of their demographic segment to enjoy the privileges and respect due to such a large group.   I intend that this report will be significant toward that process.

Chapter 2 – BRINGING BACK DEM SLAVERY DAYS

This report was initiated in 1994 as part of an extensive set of reports I called *The Police State: Amerikkka 1995*. That series detailed various aspects of the development of techniques of population management and included reports on police and military technology, recent changes in law enforcement, the judiciary, juvenile incarceration, along with other aspects of what I perceived were tactics to further the rigid management of certain segments of society. I linked it all to social engineering resulting from national security policies that were illustrative of an evolving *fascist* ideology within American politics.

The original title of this report, when released in October 1994, was *Amerikkka: The World's Biggest Prison*, and as that title indicated, by that time this country had achieved the infamous record of the highest number of jailed citizens of any country on the planet, even greater than such similarly repressive nations as South Africa, Russia, and China.

Today, some two years later, the trends toward incarceration have continued to swing further toward repression. The rate of imprisonment is particularly bitter for the *so-called* minorities within America, those of African, Native American, Puerto Rican and Latin American descent. While the main focus of this report will be on the relationship between Africans and the American prison system, much of the enclosed text will be equally as relevant to the other non-white ethnic groups, Native Americans, those Spanish-speaking members, and certain Pacific Islanders residing in the U.S.

While not wishing to trivialize the plight of other groups, it is quite a broad scope already examining the corrections system in the context of its impact on the Black community, and no one can deny that Blacks in America have disproportionately suffered under the American criminal justice system.

Note the following chart, extracted from U.S. Department of Justice figures published in June 1996, which demonstrates the racial disparity of the corrections system at yearend 1994:

- Estimated numbers of adult corrections populations, yearend 1994, in jail, state and federal prisons, parole or probation – U.S. Department of Justice, 1996

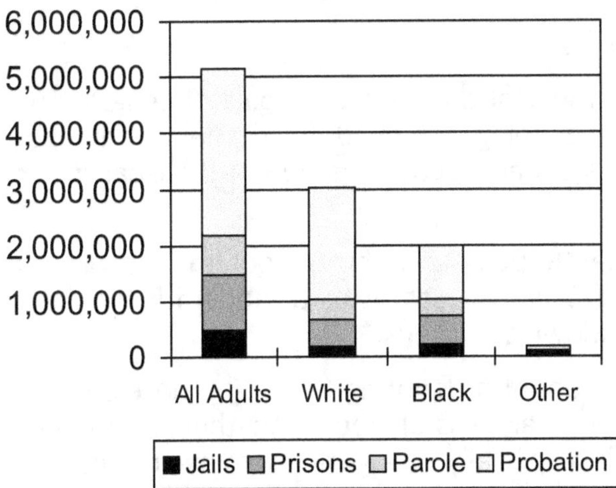

In this report, I wish to illustrate how a phenomenal increase in imprisonment, which commenced at the beginning of Ronald Reagan's presidency and reached its peak in the two years following the Bush administration, signaled a definite closure to the civil rights era. Also, in this report, I'll point out certain sub-plots such as

- the disproportion of Blacks trapped within the corrections systems of the U.S., U.K., France, and other countries;

- the harsher sentences meted out to Blacks;

- the growth of juvenile imprisonment;

- women in prison;

- jailhouse lifestyle;

- the exploitation of cheap prison labor;

- "cruel and unusual punishment;"

- the role of drugs in the rapid expansion of prison populations;

- this country's massive financial investment in prisons;

- social trends (such as poverty, miseducation, electronic media and racism), which exacerbate the crisis

- the death penalty;

- perhaps most important, the larger impact of generations of young people being removed from their traditional duties as producers and defenders within their particular community.

I will also frequently point out throughout this document how the state of California serves as a model for the *New World Order* lockdown of citizens.

This is, without a doubt a daunting task. The necessity for producing such an analysis is obvious – anything that might help Black people, especially young males, to avoid this boat which is carrying our future into a new form of bondage, is of immeasurable value. I have become aware that various of my *Conscious Rasta Reports* have been instrumental in changing people's reality and assisting large groups of people in comprehending their agenda and in bucking *the system*. That is the mission of the **Conscious Rasta Report**.

Today most of the more than 40 million Africans living in America stand on the precipice of a future in which they might end up irrelevant in policy decisions, handicapped by poverty, rigidly managed as a collective group, propagandized against as the scourge of the planet and locked in jail at the highest rate of any group in the world. The great danger within this broader trend of negatives is that we stand to lose our place in the family of humanity. Because of the deliberate policies of the U.S. national security establishment, managers of an American police state, Blacks have once again been brought to the brink of wholesale genocide.

It is thus my duty that this analysis of prisons be of tremendous value to policy strategists, community organizers, coalitions against imprisonment as well as those who've been locked down, are youth at risk or families of prisoners and to anyone conscious of the fact that high rates of imprisonment are injurious to a people's future. I trust that somewhere in this text, all of these groups should find some enlightenment in the facts as I have presented them.

According to dire prophecies, widespread imprisonment for Blacks and other *unwanted* populations in America will not only persist but worsen despite a recent reduction in crime. I will attempt to illustrate that this is a deliberate and preconceived outcome, even though the implications of documenting that *conspiracy* goes far beyond this one report. Those familiar with the *Conscious Rasta Report* are aware that I have linked these ethnic and racial policies to the larger agenda of population control in an increasingly crowded (and non-white) global reality.

Thus one could view the jailing of large numbers of reproductive-age youth from specific ethnic groups as a key toward eventually lowering the rate of childbirth within those communities. What I am proposing is that we begin to look at the move to incarcerate large numbers of a population group ultimately as a form of fertility control. Until Black leaders, as well as those who lead other ethnic groups, begin to view this wholesale jailing as deliberate social engineering, I am convinced that they will continue to promote irrelevant proposals and political agenda or, worse yet, advocate policies which are contrary to the best interests of their constituency.

Mere superstition, chasing elusive "American values," weepy handwringing or shouting at invisible ghosts won't resolve our problem. Accurate analysis linked to effective leadership, along with sufficient commitment of resources, will ultimately change our reality.

My contribution to that effort is the production of *accurate research and analysis,* and thus, without the commitment of the other aspects of this effort to change our reality, this report will provide little or nothing toward the resolution of this incarceration crisis. In the past, I have not only been called upon to provide this analysis but to function as instigator, principle worker, manager and financier of the solution. Experience has shown that it is a mistake to force a dedicated member of the analytic or academic community to take upon so many distracting tasks and is indicative that failure is likely.

In the future, if I or any other analyst produces research of significant value, and we are not backed up by the larger community, then we are doomed to failure in the short term. The profound value of this point cannot be understated. This is the way that it works with the dominant community within America. That segment of the population that is empowered, enriched, accomplishes most of its goals and operates out of their own will and not the manipulation of an external elite. They back up their researchers with the full weight of their community's resources.

Barring no radical changes, Africans in America will experience continued suffering because so much of our human resource has already been shackled, locked down, and shunted away to the fringes of society — this due to America's obsession with jails. This process must be interrupted before we can reclaim a sense of dignity and begin to raise the status of our community to enjoy the respect and privileges due to such a group. I intend that this report will be significant toward that process.

Chapter 3 – AMERICA: THE WORLD'S BIGGEST PRISON

The whole process of the jailing of vast numbers of a nation's citizens is a clear example of the level of "civilization," or lack thereof, which is present within that society. Though the United States shamelessly boasts itself as "leader of the free world" and "champion of democracy," a direct comparison between the U.S. and the prison systems of the other industrialized nations paints a radically different image. Without a doubt, America only has the brutal examples of the WWII fascist states, the excesses of Stalin's USSR, South Africa and Zionist Israel as peers in the business of internal suppression of their dissident population along with other undesired groups. The climate of crime hysteria in the U.S. will make things dramatically worse over the closing years of the millennium. The immediate future beyond the year 2000 also appears bleak if one were to use the current rate of incarceration as an indicator.

The opening quotation from Gunnar Myrdal's landmark, and influential analysis ***AN AMERICAN DILEMMA: The Negro Problem and Modern Democracy***, originally published in 1944 and re-published in 1962 by Harper and Row, confirms that the disproportionate imprisonment of persons of African descent is part of a larger strategy targeting Blacks for removal from American society. If I were to find any fault with Mr. Myrdal's quotation about mid-20th century American racial relations and their relevance to today's reality, it is with the first four words, "There is no doubt" – within a large number of persons with whom I have conversed, there *is* doubt that the dominant population would harbor such feelings of resentment toward the presence of so many Blacks within America.

America had already reached the second-highest rate of incarceration in the industrialized world with a whopping 519 of every 100,000 persons in the U.S. being locked up in 1993 (according to a September 1994 report released by **The Sentencing Project**). This rate was 22% higher than in 1989 and 5 to 8 times higher than most industrialized nations. The U.S. rate of imprisonment was exceeded only by Russia (558) and was followed by South Africa (368 under the white racist social policy of *apartheid*, before the formation of the African-majority government of Nelson Mandela. Mandela has subsequently *increased* the numbers of black South Africans who are jailed because of a rapidly increasing drug trade and subsequent increases in violent crime). This stood in stark contrast to other nations' rates such as China with 111 per 100,000 and at the other extreme, Sweden with a minuscule four citizens jailed per 100,000.

Within the criminal justice system, most of this phenomenal increase of U.S. citizens imprisoned between 1980 and 1996 can be attributed to a disastrous new combination system of stiff drug laws, mandatory minimum sentences and tight parole policies instigated during the eighties and early nineties. Certainly, the broad movement which coalesced around Ronald Reagan's "voodoo" economic and social visions was the catalyst to send this madness into overdrive. The roles of racism and class division can never be underestimated in this process. The government of George Bush further escalated the lunacy. Outside of the justice system, the reasons for the increase in imprisonment were many.

The 1994 study by The Sentencing Project, which counted a total of 1.3 million inmates in America's jail and prison systems, noted that "get-tough policies of the past two decades have failed to reduce crime". Most of the blame for the rapid increase in the rate of incarceration was attributed to stiff drug laws. Of course, statistics for drug conviction would not be this high without the persistence of high unemployment and the continued ready accessibility of *abusable* substances. The majority of inmates (over 80 percent) who are in federal prison are there for non-violent crimes. The numbers entering the nations' lockups are staggering. According to the 1994 analysis, the inmate population in the U.S. was increasing by 8.5% per year. Subsequent reports which compliment that landmark analysis from **The Sentencing Project** pose even graver projections.

For 1996 the rate of incarceration in the United States has accelerated its steady rise. The annual rate of increase in late 1994, 8.5% per year, has now climbed to 9.7% per year. With the radical changes to be expected as a result of the new federal welfare guidelines passed in 1996, combined with harsh criminal legislative efforts such as "Three Strikes" and "mandatory minimum sentence" laws, this research indicates that an alarming level of incarceration will most definitely persist for the foreseeable future.

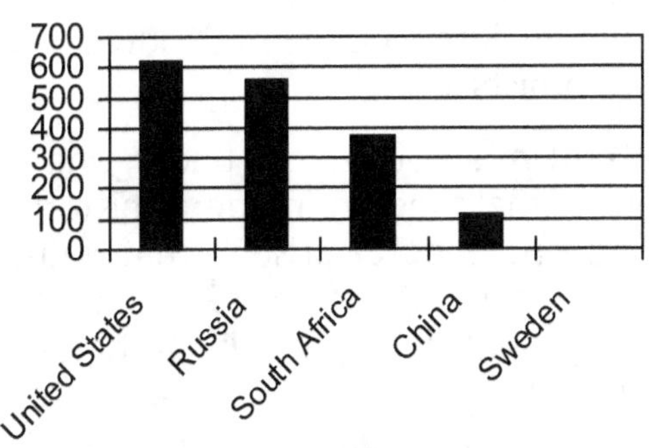

■ Imprisoned populations per 100,000 (1994)

Chapter 4 – INCREASING INCARCERATION IN THE U.S. 1980-94

Today, in 1996, the number of adults in jail or prison within America stands at 1.6 million people – *a staggering 623 of every 100,000 U.S. residents*. According to *L.A. Times* staff writer David Lamb in an article entitled "Main Street Finds Gold in Urban Crime Wave," this has led to an economic windfall for a host of investors and speculators in the rapidly growing prisons industry. Of the phenomenal growth in prison populations over the past two decades, Lamb writes:

> Although Republicans and Democrats accuse each other of being "soft on crime," the facts seem to indicate otherwise. The nation's prison and jail population, now 1.6 million, has tripled since 1980 and has grown so fast that today one in 167 U.S. residents is incarcerated. If these inmates were suddenly turned loose on the job market, the unemployment rate would jump between 1 and 2 percentage points, economists say.

According to the article, the United States has undergone a prison-building obsession unmatched in modern history. There are some 123 state and federal prisons that were either completed or under construction in 1996. Small communities are scrambling to attract a penal institution to their locale along with the lucrative contracts for construction, servicing and maintenance of the costly facilities. Also notable is the growth of profit-motivated prison operators. In a very real sense, prisons have begun to take on the image of the economic boondoggle that the defense industry assumed during the Cold War era. *Times* author Lamb points out that prisons have become a lucrative part of a $100-billion-a-year growth industry of crime-fighting. He notes that nationally, four jails open each month. The U.S. added 43,000 new beds in 1993.

States engaged in the prison-building spree are led by California, which is today in the midst of a $5.2-billion binge to construct an additional 51,000 beds. Texas is spending $1.5-billion. The bodies required to fill those beds are like chattel these days, with businesses scrambling to service the varied needs of the ever-swelling ranks of prisons, inmates, and jailers. According to all indicators, they are enjoying a lucrative investment.

A significant U.S. Department of Justice (DOJ) publication was published in June 1996 and entitled *Correctional Populations in the United States, 1994*. The report traced the expanding population within the corrections system between 1980 and 1994, the period of the most phenomenal prison growth in U.S. history. By June 1994, the U.S. had a total of 5.1 million adults who were under some form of correction. This included some 3 million adults on probation, 992,000 who were in state or federal prisons, 484,000 in local jails, and an additional 690,000 on parole. As a percentage of the nation, this 5.1 million represented 2.7% of the adult population. In contrast, in 1980 the proportion of adults in the correctional system was 1.1%. In a mere ten years, the rate of incarceration of adults in this country had *increased* one and a half times.

These rates translate to phenomenal numbers of individuals locked down or otherwise under supervision during any year in the U.S. The rapid expansion in incarceration began to occur at the beginning of the Ronald Reagan Administration in 1981. In 1980 the estimated correctional population in the U.S. was 1,840,400, of which 501,826 were in jail or prison. By 1994 those figures had exploded to 5,129,700 in the larger system, 1,475,329 of whom were in jail or prison. This represents an increase of 3,289,300 (270% higher) adults who were in probation, jail, prison or parole (increase in prisons and jails alone was 973,503 – a 294%). Later in this report, I will examine particular social trends peculiar to the Reagan and Bush presidential administrations which fed this tremendous rise in imprisonment. These same policies are currently being expanded upon under the administration of Bill Clinton.

• Adults in jail or prison in the U.S. 1980-94 – U.S. Department of Justice, 1996

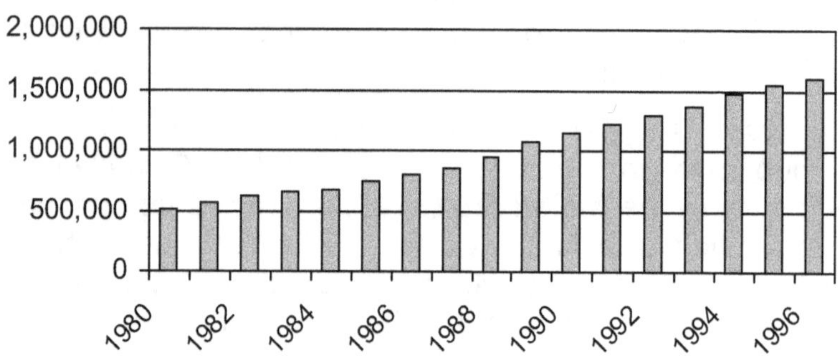

By far, the greatest increase in the jailed population for any demographic group was for African-Americans. In 1985, according to the June 1996 DOJ report, 3.7% of black adults were in jail, state or federal prison. For 1994 that percentage had swollen to 7.2%, nearly doubling in nine years. In contrast, for Whites, in 1985, one-half percent were in jail, state or federal prison. By 1994 the proportion for white adults had risen to .9%, one eighth the rate at which black adults were incarcerated. The total number of adults in the corrections system includes not only imprisoned but those on parole and probation. For 1985 estimates of 1.2% of Whites and 5.2% of Blacks under corrections were given. By 1994 those figures had increased to 1.9% of Whites and 9.1% of Blacks. [note the following graph]

- Percentage of adults in jails & prisons as well as overall corrections system by race and sex, 1994 – U.S. Dept. of Justice figures

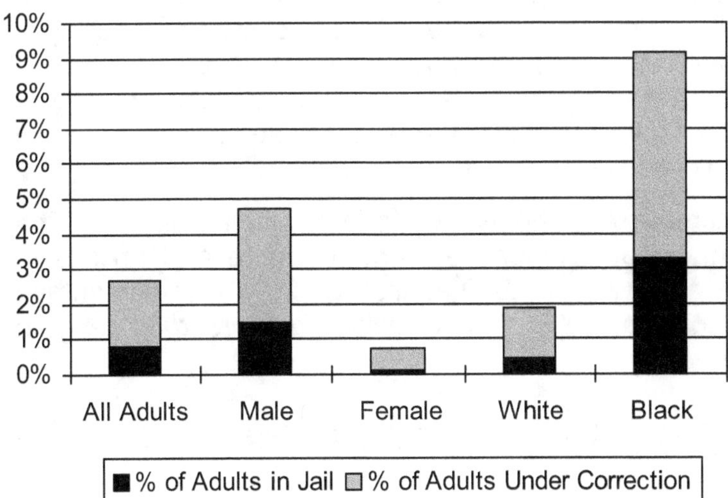

[**Note**: After no small amount of study, I have become convinced that U.S. census estimates of the total Black population have become *seriously* undercounted for the last four decades. If what I have hypothesized is true that the number of persons of direct African descent is as much as *111% higher* than published figures than this would significantly alter the rate at which Blacks are incarcerated. I personally believe this to be the case so that these escalated percentages, which are calculated upon artificially-low census estimates, should reflect much less of a shocking increase – nonetheless, there are far, far too many people who have been drawn into the penal network]

The single greatest contributors to state prisons are violent crimes, followed by property crimes, drugs and public disorder. Yet the greatest *change* which contributed to the phenomenal increase in jail numbers was people sentenced for drug violations. For prison commitments to state correctional facilities, drug offenses accounted for 6.4% of state prisoners in 1980 in contrast to 22.3% in 1994. This translates to 19,000 drug offenders in state prison in 1980 compared to 202,000 in 1994 – a whopping *increase* of 963%! When one considers that the cost of housing a prisoner in state prison averages over $20,000 per year, in some states as high as $30,000 to $50,000, it is easy to see that the expansion of prisons has paralleled the phenomenal growth of the drug trade.

This same trend holds for federal penitentiaries. The percentage of drug-offense inmates in federal prisons in 1980 was 25.2% or 4,900 adults. By 1994 that percentage was 59.2% or 51,823 individuals – *a more than ten-fold increase*!

• Growth of drug-related commitments to state & federal prisons for years 1980, 1985, 1991-94 – U.S. DOJ, 1996

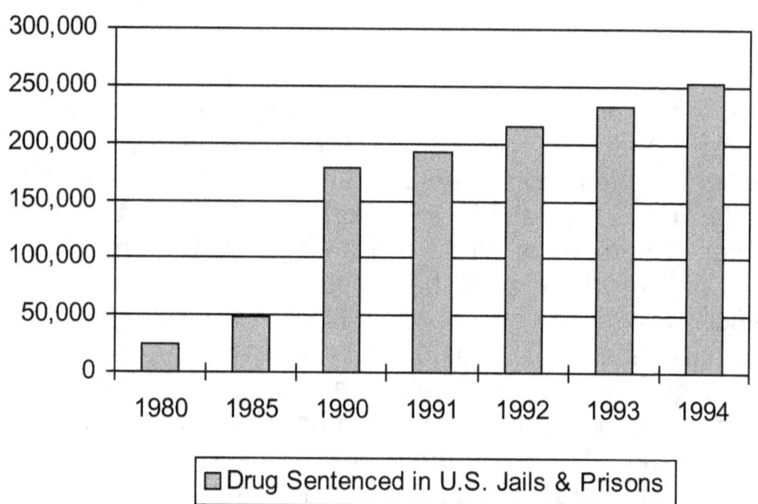

CALIFORNIA: MODEL FOR A NEW NATIONAL LOCKUP?

According to reports from late 1994, in so far as the rate of citizens in penal institutions, California, with 626 persons jailed per 100,000, fared far worse than the national average. With a current 9.5% average annual growth rate, in 1996, this figure can be expected to be near 700 per 100,000. Taken separately, California leads the world in the percentage of its citizens in jail. In 1994 there were 126,000 inmates in the California state prison system, a system designed to hold half that number. This was nearly twice as high as the second-highest state Florida with 59,000 inmates. By 1996, California's state prison population has grown to a reported 142,000 prisoners. Additionally, the states of Texas, New York, Illinois, Ohio, Michigan as well as the federal government, are significant for their large numbers of prisoners.

In addition to state prisons, California's county and city jails contributed another 74,000 or more inmates to the overall total. According to Vincent Schiraldi, executive director of the **Center on Juvenile and Criminal Justice**, "With a violent crime rate of 1,059 per 100,000, California has achieved the dubious distinction of having both the highest rate of violent crime and the highest incarceration rate in the world."

This contradiction is further evidence that the absurdity of building dozens of high-tech containment facilities along with low-tech concentration camps has never proven to lower the overall crime rate substantially. A political climate that throws vast amounts of money into more police, tougher criminal courts and prisons is a festival for lunatics. Long Beach Press-Telegram columnist Tom Hennessy uses a quotation from Albert Einstein to clearly illustrate this failure: "Insanity is doing the same thing over and over again and expecting a different result." Hennessy's October 1994 article also quoted an exasperated Orange County Superior Court Judge James Gray, " some day we will all be in a prison or working for one."

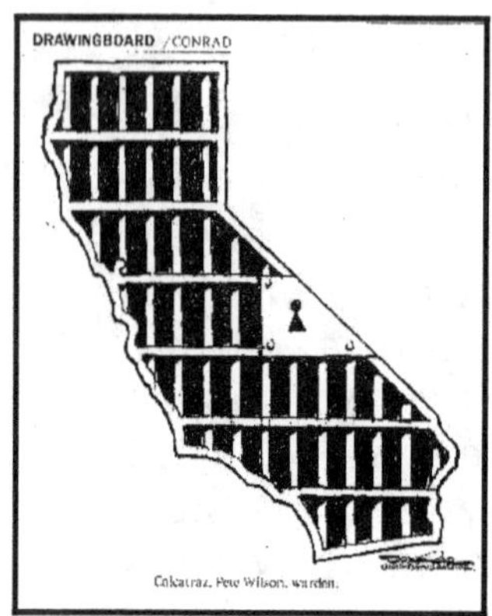

Calcatraz. Pete Wilson, warden.

The increase in the California state prison system population has, for several years, averaged a phenomenal 9.5 percent each year. In addition to being a model for the nation's rapidly expanding corrections system, the state's Department of Corrections is generally on the cutting edge of policy changes that affect the lives of inmates throughout the country.

Unfortunately, California's prison system is also an ugly model for the sorry state of race relations in the United States; as well, the system is a hotbed of gang rivalry. News frequently reports detail accounts of bloody fights between opposed gangs, often pitting Black against Hispanic, or Crips versus Bloods. Fights sometimes involve the White Aryan Brotherhood, a supremacist network spread throughout the nation's prisons. In 1996 alone, several racial melees have occurred at Pelican Bay and Corcoran as well as at other state prisons and juvenile facilities.

I had the unforgettable experience of once having been caught literally in the middle of a huge *intra*-racial melee involving as many as 200 gang-affiliated Black inmates during a *Juneteenth Day* commemoration. This occurred in 1995 at the maximum-security Lompoc Federal Penitentiary. After a harrowing half-an-hour trying to retrieve our 12-member party of visitors from the midst of this wild slugfest, we were all finally reassembled in a more secure section of the facility, ourselves temporarily locked down. We later became suspicious that the Lompoc authorities had, earlier that day, apparently anticipated a major incident. That morning while our party was waiting to clear processing to enter the prison, a truck arrived, and we witnessed the unloading of dozens of assault rifles, shotguns and revolvers which were stashed in the prison armory. We concluded that the warden or other high-level administrator had brought about the disturbance to undermine the celebration of the Black holiday commemorating the end of bondage and to stigmatize the prison's burgeoning Black consciousness movement.

The ultimate impact of the "Three Strikes" legislation on the expected rapid rise in prison populations in California is, at the time of this writing, still being debated. Between the inception of the "three strikes" law in May 1994 and October 1996, nearly 2500 inmates have been designated "three-time losers" and sentenced under the provision that mandates convicts serve minimum sentences of 25 years-to-life for their third felony conviction. Recently certain Department of Corrections officials have scaled-down estimates of how many prisoners will enter state facilities by the turn of the century. A previous projection of 230,000 for the year 2000 has now been lowered to 181,000, (still some 40,000 more than the current state population of 142,000). Analysts have attributed part of the new lowered projections to leniency by sentencing judges shown for persons up for their second strike, which under the Three Strikes law called for doubling for sentences. Some 19,600 felons have been sentenced under provisions of the law for their second conviction. Falling rates of serious crimes for 1995 and 1996 have also contributed to the lowered projections.

Chapter 5 – JUVENILE DETENTION GROWS UP

Another area where the madness within this nation's correction policy is most obvious is the tremendous number of juveniles locked down in detention facilities, doing time in boot camps, who are on probation or otherwise drawn into the web of criminal corrections. A U.S. Department of Justice (DOJ) report, released in September 1994 by the Office of Juvenile Justice and Delinquency Prevention, decried "crowded, substandard facilities that lack anti-suicide policies and adequate health screening," reported *Associated Press* on September 26.

The DOJ survey covered 984 detention centers, training schools, ranches, farms, and boot camps that held 65,000 juveniles and found that as few as 20% had sufficient bed space, healthcare, adequate security or suicide control. More than 18,000 suicide attempts and "self-mutilations" were reported in the survey as well as 24,000 attacks on other inmates and 8,000 attacks on staff. The issue of health care for juveniles under detention was notably criticized, in particular the insufficiency of staff trained to conduct health screenings.

The critical period of corrections expansion, the decades of the 1980s and 1990s, can be again be examined to provide an understanding of the explosion in youth imprisonment, which kept pace with similar growth in adult incarceration. The *L.A. Times* reported findings from a **Rand Corporation** report from June 1996 that traced the rapid rise in juvenile incarceration. Several findings of this report, along with numerous other studies that are cited herein, should provoke no small measure of alarm among anyone concerned that this country is grossly mismanaging the development of its youth. In most societies of the world, children are nurtured as the most valued segment of potential human resource. A few examples of America's tragic reality follow:

- Arrests for violent crime among 14 to 17-year olds rose 47% from 1989 to 1994, according to the Rand report; a previous study from the same group estimated that the state's "Three Strikes" legislation might be able to produce a 21% drop in serious crime in California but that it would come at a frightening price – enforcement of the law would cost *$5.5 billion per year*. Has this massive reinvestment in the imprisonment of youth paid off? Figures for juvenile arrests in 1995 *do* suggest a 2.9% drop from the previous year for violent offenders between ages 10 and 17, yet criminals acts by juveniles, such as aggravated assault, robbery, rape and murder, remain outrageously high;

- A DOJ report from August 1996 noted a decline in youth arrest rates for various categories including – 1) murder: peaking at 14.4 arrests per 100,000 in 1993, dropping to a rate of 13.2 in 1994 and 11.2 in 1995 (murder rates had grown substantially since 1983); 2) overall juvenile violent crime cases had fallen from 527 per 100,000 in 1994 to a rate of 512 in 1995; 3) in California the rate of juvenile arrests for violent crime was 656 per 100,000 in 1990, but that record rate had been reduced by 1994 to just under 622;

- The California Youth Authority operates 15 juvenile detention facilities statewide and, in scrambling to add new facilities, was in September 1996 competing with the Cal State University system for possession of the now-defunct former Camarillo State Mental Hospital's

600 acre/85 building facility. The Youth Authority is "bracing for increased populations from the upsurge in teenage violence..." and wants to convert the Camarillo facility to confinement for offenders up to age 25. The Youth Authority puts its current inmate population at 150% of the system's capacity;

- The role of gangs as a major contributing factor to the growing number of juvenile commitments cannot be under-appreciated. According to a survey conducted by James C. Howell, Ph.D., as part of an Office of Juvenile Justice and Delinquency Prevention assessment conducted in April 1994, law enforcement authorities estimate that there were in 1991, the most recent year for such figures, some 4,881 gangs in the U.S. comprising 249,324 members. For 1994 there were an estimated 46,359 reported criminal gang incidents. Local police and the FBI have reported that L.A. gangs, largely Crips and Bloods, have migrated to 45 Western and Midwestern cities. According to law officials, gang affiliation has an impact "on increases in imprisonment from the standpoint of more violent offenses, more serious injuries, and use of more lethal weapons." Gangs have also been associated with an increase in drug trafficking. Up to 90% of gang members are believed to be young with 17-years-of-age appearing to be the peak age for gang involvement;

- The quality of childcare and early-life environment, vital in the development and nurturing of youth, is under extreme pressure from a combination of factors, most notably recent federal welfare guidelines that cut funding for several significant programs. Early intervention programs, which can typically cost $10,000 per year per student, are approximately one fourth of the cost of warehousing prisoners. Yet, Early Head Start, which provides preschool to low-income children ages 3 and 4, is receiving minuscule support from the federal government, budgeting for a mere 7,400 children to enter the program between 1995 and 1997;

- It was estimated in August 1994 that the cost of jailing a juvenile in Los Angeles was $45,000 per year in contrast to $2000 per year to put a youth through a year of intervention programs. The state Office of Juvenile Justice and Delinquency Prevention, which coordinates federal, state, and local programs, has decried the commitment of such economic resources towards warehousing of inmate populations in contrast to investing in early intervention programs which have demonstrated proven success. There are more than 400 county youth lockups throughout the country. Between 1991 and 1996, some 31 of the nation's 52 boot camp programs opened in 32 states along with federal facilities. Boot camps have not been successful in reducing the rate of inmates returning into the corrections system;

- Statistics for the year 1991, provided by the DOJ Office of Juvenile Justice and Delinquency Prevention, note grossly disproportionate numbers of minorities, particularly African-American youth, caught in the criminal justice system. In 1991 about 44% of the juveniles under lockdown were Black, 34% White, and

19% Hispanic. In examining arrests for drug offenses and personal offenses, black youth were over-represented 64% and 49% respectively. The commitment of Blacks to stricter juvenile facilities was also apparent, comprising 47% of the population of the harsher training schools while only 32% of the less restrictive and less crowded private facilities. The probability that a black male under age 18 would be taken into custody was as much as five times greater than white males in certain states;

● The racial makeup of jailed juvenile population in the U.S. (1991) – U.S. DOJ 1996

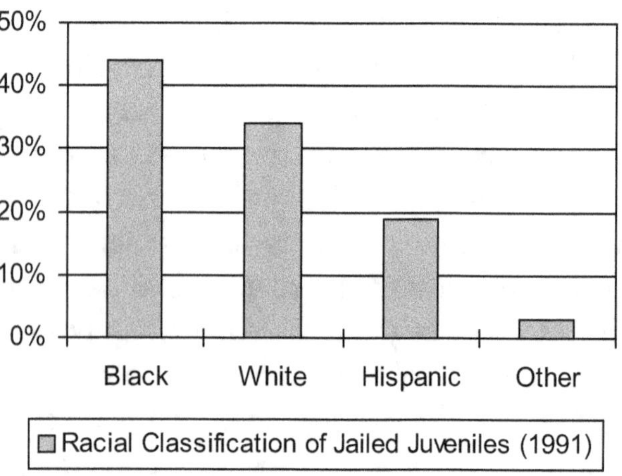

■ In June 1996, the youngest person ever charged for murder as an adult in California, a black youth from San Diego named Tony Hicks, was sentenced to 25 years to life in prison for taking the life of a 20-year-old college student, an African immigrant who was working as a pizza delivery man. Because Hicks, 14 years old at the time of the shooting, was sentenced as an adult, he will not be eligible for parole until age 36. Two other 14-year-olds involved in the murder were charged and convicted in juvenile court while an 18-year-old accomplice, also convicted in adult court, was sentenced to life in prison with no possibility of parole. Hicks was the first child tried under a then-new state law which lowered the age for which murder suspects could be charged as adults from 16 down to 14 years of age;

- President Bill Clinton's 1994 legislation, the **Violent Crime Control and Law Enforcement Act** contained provisions for trying juveniles as young as 13 in federal court as adults for violent crimes such as murder, assault, robbery, and rape. While anyone would certainly deplore such behavior by children, nonetheless, this is further evidence that America, as a society, is barbaric toward its wayward children. This nation has to acknowledge that its policies created, sustained and expanded the miserable social conditions by which so many youths have become so ruthless. Upon examining the broad impact of juvenile corrections along with the shocking expansion of the system over the past two decades, in particular its disproportionate effect on minority youth, one could determine that the immediate future looks bleak for this country, especially within inner-city communities.

Chapter 6 – WOMEN IN PRISON

For women as with the other segments of the population, the statistics for imprisonment have also reflected terrible growth. Though women are far less a proportion of the whole correctional population, about 15% of the total of 5,129,700 under incarceration (in jail, state or federal prison, parole, or probation). Growth over the last two decades in the number of adult females under correction has mirrored that for the larger society.

The U.S. Department of Justice places the number of female adults under correction for year's end 1994 at 762,200. This figure stands as nearly 1 out of 7 of the total of the overall population under correction. The number of imprisoned adult females in the U.S. during 1994 was 105,800. The number of women in jail during a critical period of expansion between 1985 and 1994 rose from 40,600 to 102,700 – an overall increase of 152%.

The ratio of incarcerated females was 53% white to 47% black in 1985 and 49% white to 51% black in 1994. Yet when one looks at the *rate of incarceration* as it differed between white and black women for December 1994, the white woman had a 1 in 1667 (.06%) chance of being in jail while, according to the DOJ, the black woman had a 1 in 230 (.44%) chance – *more than a seven-fold risk of becoming incarcerated.*

- Estimated numbers of U.S. adult women jailed and under a correctional system 1985-94 – U.S. DOJ June 1996

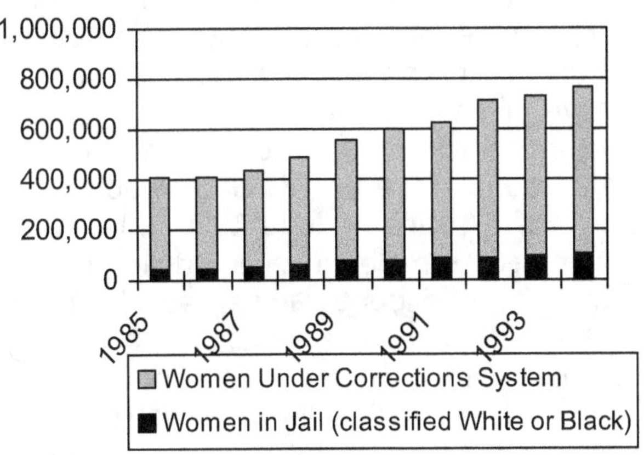

The incidence of lockdown for California women increased dramatically during the "Reagan Decade." Between 1980 and 1991, according to a report from the **Center of Juvenile and Criminal Justice**, California's male prison population rose by 153%. In contrast, the increase among women inmates was nearly double the men's rate at 289%. California's 1994 population of 7,900 women in state prison is expected to increase by an estimated 65% throughout the rest of the decade. This represents a state-sponsored assault against the family that is unparalleled throughout the industrialized world.

The network which draws large numbers of young women into the criminal justice system is particularly adept at trapping youth from the so-called inner city. Administrators, researchers, social scientists, and educators attribute this rise to harmful influences that disproportionately affect urban youth such as violence, peer influence from neighborhood gangs, dysfunctional parents, the drug trade, failing educational standards, materialism, widespread unemployment, and general rebellion against authority. Within that mix, we cannot ignore entertainment media.

For juvenile women, the growth of boot camps, mostly still an experimental process, is presently a significant area of expansion, especially since, in the 1970s and 1980s, there were so few girls in such serious trouble. Still, the notion that rigid military-style authoritarianism will succeed where other institutions have failed is asking for miracles – it may be impossible to return things to a time of simpler virtues. **Rand Corporation** researcher Peter W. Greenwood was quoted in the fourth of a series of June 1996 *L.A. Times* articles which examined female juvenile delinquency. Greenwood said that juvenile boot camps have become popular, "apparently satisfying the need to be both humanitarian and tough...[though] few if any corrections practitioners believe that strict discipline and harsh living conditions on their own will lead to lasting behavioral changes."

A significant number of women caught in the system are there because of drug addiction and mental illness. It must be emphasized that, even though drug addiction is treated in this country as a male crisis when legal drugs like pills, tranquilizers, and psychotropic drugs are analyzed for abuse, women are at *higher* risk for drug addiction. Alcohol and cocaine, especially crack, further exasperate the problem when often-reoccurring pregnancies occur. Thus the crisis includes not only addiction, criminal activity and correction but the added burdens of motherhood complicate every aspect of the crisis.

Increasingly harsh legal measures are being implemented by state legislatures, such as pushing for laws that criminalize giving birth to drug-addicted babies. Courts frequently remove children from the custody of mothers drawn into the criminal justice system. There even exists a historical record of government agencies forcing women to undergo chemical or surgical sterilization. Prison authorities increasingly ignore the role of mental illness in the behaviors of women in jail, and drug addiction is treated as a criminal problem as opposed to a health crisis.

A report in the June 1996 magazine *Archives of General Psychiatry* raises the alarm that nearly 80% of 1,272 women detained in jail awaiting trial had a history of mental illness, and some 70% had exhibited such behavior within the last six months. Another report by a North Carolina-based researcher found symptoms of mental illness in 44% of 885 female felons she studied. Alcohol and drug addiction were mainly at fault complicated by "borderline personality disorders."

The disproportionate targeting of non-white women for prosecution over drug cases has drawn protest, albeit rather minuscule. It must be noted that large numbers of suburban or wealthy-class women can successfully conceal the effects of drug addiction while obtaining their drug supply from the safe and discreet environment of a series of posh doctors' offices. As such, women from these groups have been mainly immune to criminal prosecution.

In general, if more privileged individuals find themselves in legal trouble over their addiction, they nearly always have the available option to check themselves into treatment and avoid jail sentences. This is not the case for the vast numbers of women whose domestic or economic situation would require them to seek subsidized public services. Such services, if capable, are hopelessly over-taxed and far too few to service the massive numbers in need. Thus an increasing number of women have become mired in the revolving door of the criminal justice system.

Increasingly women are being treated with much more severity than in previous decades – one notoriously ruthless sheriff in Arizona even bragged at being the first jailer in the United States to shackle females together, five at a time, and send them out on road gangs to perform cleanup work.

Chapter 7 – JAILHOUSE CORRESPONDENCE

Over the years, I have collected correspondence from dozens of men and women in prisons throughout the country (among my collection, of which I take great pride, is one entry from one of my heroes – Yahweh ben Yahweh, who wrote from Pennsylvania). I've always tried to respond to each letter as circumstances would allow. From these letters, I have gotten a sense of the frustration that Brothers and Sisters are feeling because of their current lockdown. Many of them are quite good at conveying their thoughts on paper. I make it a point not to inquire as to the offenses for which they were convicted.

I do my best to always mail some published reading material to those letters I respond to, usually sending a few prints of the many articles I have written. Occasionally I'll post books, cassettes, videos – whatever I can spare at the time, and the recipients always love getting such items – when they make it through censorship. Occasionally some materials are blocked by prison authorities. Much depends on the security level of the facility where they're imprisoned and the strictness of the policies of administrators. Some of the restrictive policies which frustrate the process include a ban on certain types of politically-oriented material, packaging requirements (i.e., cassettes must be shrink-wrapped), potentially "provocative" content (one cassette was rejected because it had a brief reference to the trial of O.J. Simpson), and origin of the material.

Several of the inmates with whom I corresponded became extremely frustrated with what they determined to be particularly antagonistic behavior from judicial and correction authorities on themselves, including restricting participation in progressive organizations.

One such brother, incarcerated at Allenwood Federal Correctional Institute at White Deer, Pennsylvania, wrote me a poignant letter in July 1994. He expressed deep frustration with the federal Department of Justice regarding what was, according to his analysis, deliberate and systematic racist oppression against Black inmates by the U.S. judicial system. In his correspondence to me, he forwarded a three-page letter addressed to "Mr. President." It is a moving and eloquent letter, which I believe speaks for a lot of brothers and sisters in the system, and so I would like to share a portion of it:

Dear Mr. President:

May peace be upon you, and the guidance of the One God. It is my hope that this letter arrives to find you, your family and your staff doing well. This is a follow-up letter to the letters written [to] you previously concerning the flagrant excesses of the United States Parole Commission, in conjunction with certain members of the Federal Bench, vented against the legitimate rights and expectations of African (Black) Americans in the status of parolees.

Since somewhere around the mid-eighties, the U.S. Parole Commission has deliberately pursued a policy of routinely violating the statutory and constitutional, civil and citizenship rights of the Africans (Blacks) held captive under their sway. They have deliberately pursued a course of action that is patently illegal. It should be noted that the complained about action of the U.S. Parole Commission actually began around the same time that the U.S. Congress enacted the overly harsh and absolutely discriminative laws, crack and otherwise, directed at the lives of Africans (Blacks) in this United States of America, (see attached exhibit 1). The combined actions of the U.S. Parole Commission and the U.S. Sentencing Committee, with the explicit or implied approval of the U.S. Congress, seem to indicate a concerted effort by the officials of this U.S. government to usurp and impugn the legitimate and constitutional rights of Africans (Blacks) by exposing us to cruel and unusual punishments; the curtailment of due process rights; the arbitrary and capricious application of the law; and, the deliberate violation of U.S. Supreme court decisions, and other precedent law, when confronted with Africans (Blacks) who have been perceived to have violated the law, especially as it appertains to Blacks in the status of parolees.

...[T]he litany of illegal conduct by the U.S. Parole Commission, with the help and support of the federal judges and magistrates, reaches much deeper into an area of treatment that is prohibited and contrary to the rule of law in the United States of America. Is there a double-standard of law being applied discriminatively to Africans (Blacks) in the United States of America? Is the Executive Department of this government supporting and directing the onslaught of the U.S. Parole Commission and the U.S. judicial system upon the legitimate and legal rights of African (Black) men and women in the United States, especially those, such as myself, who are in the status of parolees?

...The U.S. Parole Commission must not be allowed to continue to violate parolees' freedoms without due process of the law, both substantive and procedural, as they have been in the habit of doing with impunity. They must not be allowed to continue to hold hearings <u>without</u> providing adverse witnesses, documentary evidence, etc., and ignoring the rule of law in regards to the finding of guilt or innocence!

...Justice is being routinely denied! Africans (Blacks) are being routinely discriminated against! I urge you to take steps to remedy this matter! Justice delayed, is justice denied!

Respectfully, Jeffrey M. Hill

Chapter 8 – THE EXPLOITATION OF CHEAP PRISON LABOR

Individual correctional facilities boast of vocation programs such as furniture making, print and upholstery shops, forest camps, manufacturing jobs, and other productive opportunities. Yet 40% of the inmates of California have no such activities to keep them occupied. According to the *L.A. Times,* on October 17, 1994, at that time, there were only 71,500 work assignments available to the then-current 126,000 state inmates. More than 40,000 inmates were either deemed unfit for duty or uninterested.

For their labors, California's *Prison Industry Authority* employees' average compensation was a paltry 50 cents an hour. Inmates on fire crews received 95 cents an hour. A federal class-action suit filed in October 1994 contended that such amounts paid to prison employees violated federal minimum wage laws. A victory by the inmates could cost states such as California millions of dollars in back labor and future wages. Presently laws in most states, including California, discourage prison-manufactured commercial goods from competing on the open domestic market. There exists a booming market for corporations to contract out services to prison industries. There are few if any restrictions barring the marketing of prison-labor consumer goods for export, a practice for which a hypocritical U.S. government and news media frequently castigate nations such as China. A California prison-made product known as *Gangsta Blues* denim jeans is marketed in Japan, a country which, quipped a marketing director for Prison Industries, "has a kind of fascination with crime in California. It's kind of strange."

Ignoring the very practices of the federal government and states such as California, Texas, Georgia and Alabama which utilize a significant prison labor force, California's zealous governor Pete Wilson signed into law in September 1996 a bill making California the first state to outlaw purchases of goods produced in foreign slave-labor camps. The largely symbolic law "is intended to build economic pressure against exploitative foreign factories in such countries as India, Pakistan and Brazil, as well as China." Touted as an "anti-slavery" law, this is the epitome of hypocrisy on the part of persons like California's governor. Pete Wilson issued a press release at the signing of the bill that stated, "Unfortunately, the practice of forced, slave or convict labor is not uncommon in our world... These violations of humanity will not be tolerated. If you do business with a company that uses child or slave labor, you will not do business with the state of California."

In response, a spokesman at China's consulate in San Francisco refuted allegations that his nation exports goods manufactured by prisoners and dismissed such accusations as groundless. Wang Yusheng stated that "China strictly prohibits the export of products made by prison labor" due to a longtime economic agreement with the U.S. While the U.S. media has long been a harsh critic of China's human rights policies, it should be noted that America locks up its citizens at over five times the rate as China and conditions within American jails are much more savage then corresponding conditions within China. Compared to U.S. prisons, China's confinement facilities would mostly qualify as minimum-security lockups. (While not diminishing the impact of the estimated 1.37 million unfortunate Chinese incarcerated, when one compares the criminal justice system of the United States to any other industrialized nation, the barbarity and money-driven nature of this country's prison system leaves little room for America's castigation of *anyone*.)

In contrast to California, Oregon has no restrictions barring domestic marketing of prison-made goods. It's more lucrative to all. According to an October 17, 1994, *L.A. Times* article by Dan Morain, "Oregon prisoners make up to $7 per hour, they pay taxes, give 5% to a victims fund, 5% to family support, 50% for room and board and put 25% into savings."

Morain goes on to detail a program, sponsored by then-California Gov. George Deukmejian and approved by voter initiative, called Joint Ventures. Through the program, inmates at Folsom Prison make neon signs for hospitals and casinos; San Quenton inmates bake cookies; other facilities conduct such enterprises as a pig farming or recycling garbage. Yet, despite opportunities for employment, current and proposed laws have the prisoner working in a state of indentured servitude. There was some merit to what rap artist Sistah Soljah shouted on her 1992 Sony Records release, *360 Degrees of Power* – Soljah proclaimed that America has begun "The Final Solution...Slavery's Back in Effect":

President's Announcement:

Good evening America. This is your President. Please listen carefully to the announcement I'm about to make. After careful consideration and research, Vice President Duke, Congress and myself have concluded that Black people have not advanced technologically. Their educational testing scores are on a rapid decline. The vast majority of them are on welfare and producing babies at a faster rate than they can support them. We will not carry them anymore. We are left with no choice but to put slavery back into effect.

All Blacks will report to the designated camps in their area to receive further orders. The only Blacks excused will be those serving in the United States Army and the Police. Any Blacks who do not cooperate will be terminated immediately. I repeat, slavery's back in effect.

Chapter 9 – HUNTING SEASON: Prison Shootings by Officers

Another dismal record for California, according to the State Department of Justice records from 1983 to date in 1994, state prison officers killed more inmates than the nations' seven next-largest prison systems *added together*. The figure for California during this period, 36 deaths, is *more than three times the combined total of the next seven states*. A deadly spree of such shootings, which caused 27 deaths as well as scores of wounding by gunfire, occurred from 1989 to 1994, and every one of these prison guard killings has been ruled justifiable by California State Department of Correction officials.

Justifiable homicide in these cases includes numerous episodes of bullets that "go astray" and kill individuals not only not involved in the ill-fated disturbance, but many who had the reputation of model prisoners as well as respected inmate activists.

Though a tiny percentage of the shootings were prosecuted as criminal homicide, no correction officers have been convicted of a criminal offense. Part of the reason for the failure to effectively discipline officers who irresponsibly shoot inmates has been that record-keeping has been so terribly slack. According to an October 24, 1994, article in the *Orange County Register*, correction officials are not sure "how many times it happens (shootings of inmates)." The report noted, "when a fatal shooting occurs, the primary investigation is handled by correctional staff assigned to the institution." A case of the fox guarding the henhouse?

According to the article, "from 15 to 20 percent of all shootings at Pelican Bay from 1990 to late 1993 were not examined by review boards, so said Vincent Nathan, a corrections consultant who serves as a 'special master' overseeing Texas prisons' compliance with federal court orders. "Many of the California incident reports had been altered in an attempt to conceal details that might incriminate officers."

One corrections officer, Moses Guerrero, who was responsible for the shooting death of inmate-activist Anthony 'Angry Bear' Nieto in June 1988, testified [at a corrections department hearing] that he had fired his weapon more than 100 times in eight years on the job. In the case of Nieto's murder, Guerrero and other California State Prison Sacramento officers falsified data, covered up details of the incident, and ultimately were found guilty of violating Angry Bear Nieto's civil rights. Despite a jury award of $173,000 to the family of the victim, no criminal charges were filed against Guerrero or other prison authorities.

Chapter 10 – A BILLION DOLLAR PRISON-BUILDING BOOM

Conflicting reports estimate that California spent between $2.7 and $4 billion in 1994 on the state prison system – somewhere in the range of $20,000 to 25,000 a year per inmate. This stands in direct contrast to the $4,569 the state spent that year per student in the public school system. Another area of increasing expenses, healthcare for geriatric prisoners, whose numbers will substantially rise under "Three Strikes" provisions, raises the cost of incarceration of older inmates to over $60,000.

A coalition of investment firms, money managers, political action groups, construction firms, prisons-for-profit industries, and opportunists of lessor ilk, has coalesced to lead California and the rest of the nation into this malicious obsession for more penal institutions. Three Strikes signals a gold rush fever to these investors over the coming decade. Similar laws in Washington state, Georgia and Michigan are forcing vast numbers of prisoners into the system for lengthy commitments.

A revealing series of articles appeared in the *Los Angeles Times* October 16 -19, 1994. Reporting on the massive prison-building phenomenon in the United States, writer Dan Morain quotes state Sen. Robert Presley (D-Riverside) who quipped "We call it our Pentagon around here. We say that because it costs so much. It's like the military."

Indeed, we should recall that at the end of his presidency Dwight Eisenhower warned the nation of a looming "military-industrial complex" created as a consequence of the 1947 National Security Act, enacted by his predecessor in the White House, Harry Truman. That law created the Central Intelligence Agency and set in motion the Cold War mentality. The result of this was an alliance between the

Pentagon and industry that has nearly bankrupted America in the forty-odd years since Ike's stern warning, in addition to justifying immeasurable anti-Communist posturing.

One can easily sense a similarity within anti-crime hysteria: a "lock em up throw away the key" mentality; the rush to complete containment facilities – it's easy to see that this may be the straw that breaks the back of any chance at real social progress. Anti-crime political posturing and rhetoric become even more blustery during the heat of election campaigns.

The *Long Beach Press-Telegram* on August 12, 1994, in an article entitled "Prisons: California's Growth Industry" by John Jacobs, reported that from 1852 to 1984, only 12 prisons were built in California. In the ten years between 1984 and 1994, 16 new prisons were built along with several minimum-security camps. This represented an increase of 40,524 high-security prison cells. During that decade, in California alone, over $5 billion was spent on planning, engineering, and construction of new prisons, and the resultant bond debt will double that figure when interest payments are equated into the final expenditures.

The estimated cost of adding new *maximum-security* prison cells in 1994 exceeded $113,000 per unit in the state of California and $85,000 per unit in the federal prison system. California's rate of $60,000 per *minimum-security* cell was twice the national average. Thus, in the next year and a half, according to the *L.A. Times'* October 1994 series of articles, Texas was expected to spend $1.5 billion to add 80,000 cells. In 1996, news reports reveal that the completion of L.A. County's new 1800 bed Twin Towers lockup cost $373 million – a whopping $205,000 per bed!

The reports predicted California's cost to add six new prisons, 28,000 new cells that Governor Pete Wilson had requested, was expected to exceed $2 billion. According to an October 1996 *L.A. Times* article by David Lamb, the state has committed 5.2 billion dollars to add another 51,000 beds. Thus one can examine in these news reports that over two years, the state's ambitious prison construction effort more than doubling in expense and nearly doubling in new capacity.

Small cities and rural counties are vying for bonds and other measures to attract lucrative prisons. Not only do the cities gain service contracts for prisons in their economies, but the large complexes generate tax revenues, provide a payroll increase for residents, attract new businesses to service the expanding labor pool, and attract light-manufacturing as well as other prison service industries to the area. Corrections staff are a welcome group to community life. For the foreseeable future, prisons are expected to be a recession-proof industry.

Another disturbing item about the prison cell boom is that it is generating inequality in the conditions by which some serve their sentences. This partly exists based upon some more fortunate people's ability to shell out anywhere from $55 to $78 per night to serve time in the relative comfort of suburban jail facilities, the cost of a moderately priced hotel room. A few entrepreneurial police and sheriff's departments have constructed facilities that service "pay-to-stay" programs. According to the *L.A. Times*, October 1996, the Los Angeles suburb of Pasadena has "the largest and probably most coveted" program in which hundreds of inmates serve their time each year. Their facility reportedly brings some $130,000 income into the police department's coffers.

The pay-to-stay facility is being viewed as more comfortable and less threatening than county jails, where awareness among fellow prisoners of certain types of crimes can bring violence down upon the head (or other body parts) of the convict. Also, this type of lockup is more desirable for inmates who are on "inmate worker" status. As such, they spend part of their day at their place of employment and serve jail time in the evenings and on weekends. Such facilities can also allow celebrities to serve their jail time in an environment where they will not be forced to share too much intimate space with the "great unwashed." Thus, Pasadena's most famous inmate, who also served as an inmate worker, was Death Row Records' recording artist/producer Dr. Dre (Andre Young), who was serving time for violation of probation over an assault conviction for breaking the jaw of another rap producer.

As of February 1994, there were 27 state-run prisons and minimum-security camps in California. Another 12 prisons were already in the construction phase before the state's "Three Strikes" law was passed that year. At current funding, California can be expected to have at least 40 prisons functioning by the end of the decade. Under the Three Strikes law, it has been estimated that another 41 prisons will be needed for a total of 81 prisons holding 341,000 prisoners.

In addition to the high costs of constructing the new jail cells, a substantial budget-buster has been the high wages and benefits paid to California's corrections officers who are forced to police a prison population that increased by 420% in 15 years. Prison employment in the state increased during the last ten years by 22,000, about one employee per four inmates. Annual operating budgets for the state's prisons rose during the period from $730 million to more than $3 billion. The proportion of the state operating budget spent on prisons went from 3% in 1984 to more than 7.5% in 1994. Even more alarming, this annual budget for operating expenses is projected to increase by $645 million each year.

One example of such investment is the controversial L.A. County Twin Towers Jail. This facility is located on the east side of downtown Los Angeles and was completed in 1995 but has never been opened because of a massive deficit in the county's operating budget. After county officials had balked at the projected $100 million annual budget for the facility, predicting that its operation would require a drastic cut in patrols by deflecting deputies to staff Twin Towers, in the fall of 1996 L.A. County Sheriff Sherman Block came up with a plan to open the prison. His plan, which has raised a measure of controversy among county officials and the press, projected an annual operating budget of $75 million for the 1,818-bed facility. This is in addition to the $373 million it required to construct Twin Towers.

Thus this yet unused monument to America's obsession with jails was built at the cost of over $205,000 per bed and is projected to operate at an annual expense exceeding $41,000 per bed. The county process reported 200,000 arrest cases each year.

Such innovations as lethal electrified fencing, currently budgeted at nearly $20 million, intended to cut down on escapes and lower the cost of staffing, are also adding to the cost of prison construction. Other high-technology innovations that fail or break down lead to costly repairs, frequently running into tens of millions of dollars.

Another area of rapidly rising costs for California's prison system is the number of geriatric prisoners, whose ranks will surely swell as a result of the "Three Strikes" legislation. They included in 1994 some 200 acute care patients, more than 1000 long-term nursing care inmates, and another 3000 being treated for mental illnesses. Figures for the number of HIV/AIDS and tuberculosis-diagnosed prisoners have been challenging to access, but undoubtedly, the ratio far surpasses that of the larger society.

Given the massive investments in building, maintaining, staffing and servicing the burgeoning state prison system, it is no wonder why financial analysts have trumpeted "Go west young man and grow up with California's prison system." Between design and construction contracts, staff wages, bond dividends, management contracts, supply and delivery systems, healthcare, and other expenses involved in such massive incarceration, there is ample room for the aggressive entrepreneur to cash in. A massive media-driven crime hysteria has fueled a repressive police-state mentality within America that translates into big bucks.

The rise of the "prison-for-profit" industry has been significant since its reintroduction in 1984. An increasing number of corporations are competing for lucrative contracts to warehouse convicts. A revealing article in one of our favorite research journals, *CovertAction Quarterly*, was published in the fall 1993 issue, entitled "Private Prisons: Profits of Crime." The article noted the rush to get into the prison-for-profit business by profit-driven corporations.

A subsidiary of the Wackenhut global security conglomerate, Wackenhut Corrections Corporation at the time, controlled some 11 facilities in five states which housed 5,500 inmates. Other major prison players include the Kentucky-based U.S. Corrections Corporation, Nashville's Pricor, Leavonworth's Corrections Corporation of America, and the construction giant Bechtel Corporation.

Further fueling the nation's investment in imprisonment, the Clinton-sponsored Crime Control Act of 1994 committed $9.85 billion toward prisons, including $7.9 billion for state prison grants and $1.8 billion to reimburse states for the incarceration of undocumented immigrants. Under the bill, the state of California would thus receive 629 million dollars for prison grants, including military-style boot camps. That amount could be doubled if the state meets the "truth in sentencing" clause within the bill that requires second-time violent offenders to serve a minimum of 85% of their sentences. Other "discretionary grants" could find their way into the prison system, such as funds for AIDS programs.

Without a doubt, the collapse of this nation's social network and subsequent push toward incarceration is among the more phenomenal and disturbing trends in the industrialized world. Racial minorities are targeted for grossly disproportionate treatment within the criminal justice system. Young black males serve as fuel for this profit-driven machine to no small degree. In many ways the current trend toward widespread bondage creating windfall profits mirrors to a large extent the mercantile fortunes extracted from the previous enslavement of Africans and the accompanied destruction of this land's native population.

Chapter 11 – CRUEL AND UNUSUAL: Inhumane Prison Life

California's incarceration facilities range from minimum-security Level I forestry camps to Level IV high-containment prisons such as Pelican Bay, near the Oregon border. There, conditions are so brutal they nearly defy description, prompting four killings by officer-gunfire in its first five years of operation. Another California maximum-security facility with such a reputation is Corcoran State Prison, located in the San Juaquin Valley in the central part of the state. Since its completion in 1988, it has developed a brutal reputation similar to that of Pelican Bay.

L.A. Times writer Mark Arax's, in an extensive article, provided a shocking profile of the high-tech facility through the eyes of a surprising group of participant/observers – that of five officers, including captains and lieutenants who broke ranks and exposed the vile behaviors being committed by the staff at Corcoran. What Arax wrote in the article, entitled "Tales of Brutality Behind Bars, almost sounds unreal:

> It was common practice, they say, for guards to pair off rivals like roosters in a cockfight, complete with spectators and wagering, then sometimes shoot those who wouldn't stop fighting. Shackled inmates arriving from other prisons were pummeled by officers in an intimidation rite called "greet the bus," they say. , Other inmates were forced to stand without shoes on scorching asphalt, their severe burns blamed on games of "barefoot handball.

> ...Gunfire was ringing out nearly every day and many of these shootings were not justified," said Steve Rigg, a lieutenant at Corcoran from 1988 to 1994 who is one of several officers cooperating with the

> FBI. "The fighters posed no imminent and serious harm to each other." And sometimes, he added, "the wrong inmate was killed by mistake."

The article appears to be a legitimate piece of research (despite the *L.A. Times'* reputation for the occasional grand deception, i.e., their *anti*-CIA/crack cocaine series of articles which made an unimpressive attempt to discredit the 1996 news story that has the Black community up in arms). Thus, I sense certain credibility in these revelations, along with dozens of other complaints lodged against the state and the administrators of these notorious facilities. Arax goes on in the lengthy exposure to describe a history of brutality and barbarism directed against the hardest prisoners in the California system, of "bad shootings" and extensive moves to cover them up. An inquiry by the FBI, in over two years of direct access to the evidence of the case, has yet to produce any indictments of prison officials for violating prisoners' rights. The investigation failed to unmask Corcoran as the most barbaric of the state's 32 prisons.

In addition to such brutality, it has become evident through dozens of documented revelations from across the country that many inmates are physically abused in human experimentation. I have well-documented accounts of prisoners having been fed drug-contaminated food, used as guinea pigs in dangerous and unethical human experimentation, are subjected to medical intervention without informed consent, to include sterilization. Radioactive isotopes, castrating chemicals, addictive and bio-behavioral drugs have been covertly administered to inmates. This occurs within state, federal, and military prisons. Over this century, reports have surfaced of hundreds, perhaps thousands of prisoners having been sterilized or castrated, of which only a small percentage were offered the practice as part of a bargain.

Rumors persist that patients in prison infirmaries are injected with *AIDS-causing* chemicals. Widespread news reports exposed government-sponsored tests on humans with radiation, biological and chemical warfare agents, diseases, and other toxic research. When the stories surfaced in the fall of 1993, it was indeed confirmed that numbers of prisoners had repeatedly been administered potentially deadly substances without their knowledge or approval. Thus, this would lend a measure of credibility to the claim that among the first to become AIDS-diagnosed in the late seventies, some 200 were inmates in federal prisons located near the Army's Ft. Dietrick biological warfare research facility at Frederick, Maryland. Despite denials from numerous government spokesmen and repeated accusations that Blacks are being "overly conspiratorial," a significant number of people, from every ethnic group within America, have viewed such allegations as credible.

Another concern is that special interest groups fueled by anti-crime hysteria in the media have attempted within state legislatures to restrict and repeal inmates' limited remaining civil or human rights. The California state Senate voted in April 1994 to repeal the "bill of rights" for state inmates, enacted two decades ago, which critics assert "grants criminals too many privileges," such as first amendment protections. Thus, certain privileges as conjugal visits, family visitations, access to published literature, the right to maintain their personal property, to freely market inmate's articles and other literary works, to establish separate inmate trust funds and other "minimum human rights privileges" – these are being attacked. These assaults on inmates' liberties are yielding increasingly bizarre new legal mandates on prisoners by reactionary legislatures.

Yet as one reader reminded the *Long Beach Press-Telegram* in response to a previous letter writer's comment that "I know nothing of prison living conditions," Bruce Derrickson wrote the following revealing paragraphs:

There are no weight rooms, TVs, or three meals a day. There are weights and benches in the yard, but they are rusty and old, and they are totally gang-controlled; to use them, you join the gang or pay; TV must be provided by an outside source (relative, friend, etc.) and must meet strict prison regulations.

"Three meals a day" slopped on a plate is tasteless and repetitive, and you have 10 minutes to eat it. Any infraction of the rules by anyone means lockdown for all, and they don't let you out for lunch; you do without.

Many inmates have no outside contacts and are totally alone: no letters, no phone calls, no holiday cards, no TV, no box of decent things to eat every three months. These are the men who must join groups to survive. Cigarettes sell for $10 each, you use them to get to the phone, the doctor, an aspirin, a decent cellmate, extra food at chow time, you name it.

Despite the occasional publication of such accounts, victims' organizations condemn inmate privileges such as conjugal visits between husband and wife as "sex at taxpayer expense," and they scream for more draconian measures of punishment to be heaped on prisoners. They rail against what they view such amenities as health-club weight rooms, three meals a day, cable television, and educational opportunities. These are, in their reality, deemed as grotesque excesses lavished on the undeserving. Yet, direct testament from those imprisoned expresses significantly different opinions of the "gross excess" of prison amenities. Former inmates might claim that few in the outside world would tolerate such facilities as are made available to prisoners, even if they were for free.

Among the more bizarre pieces of legislation to have made it through the California state legislature, in September 1996, Gov. Pete Wilson signed into law a "chemical castration" bill which mandated for certain sex offenders to undergo weekly injections of the synthetic hormone Depo-Provera. A controversial woman's birth control drug, Depo-Provera blocks the production of the hormone testosterone, which is the predominant male hormone – thereby reducing a man's sex drive. A leading researcher for the noted research university at Johns Hopkins in Baltimore, Dr. Fred Berlin criticized the legislation as reactionary and not well-thought-out, stating "This [law] hasn't been done out of collaboration between medical and science people and the criminal justice system...we realize that we can't treat all criminals – the bank robber, the pedophile, the murderer – the same way." Depo-Provera has amassed a long record of adverse effects on women. It is linked to irregular bleeding, weight gain, headaches, leg cramps, depression, hot flashes, insomnia, blood clots, hypertension, increased risk of stroke, increased rate of breast and uterine cancers, and gender-mutating effects on developing fetuses. The new law mandates that men undergo a regimen that delivers a dosage *nearly 500 times more potent* than that given women as a contraceptive.

The net result of this type of *mean-spiritedness* is that this will likely only further exacerbate deep-seated inmate social pathology and increase the long-term risk to the public when such a resentful prisoner finally does make it back into society. Other alarming proposals, such as the vindictive (and morally unjustifiable) victim's compensation laws enacted by California and a handful of other states, make those convicted of certain crimes virtual *slaves-for-life* to their adjudged victims – a perilous proposal considering the record of persons *wrongfully* convicted in America. As the O.J. Simpson civil court proceeding (which is commencing in late October 1996 as I write) demonstrates, even if a person can gain a legal acquittal of felonious crimes, statutes allow vengeful groups to pursue *indentured servitude* for that individual and to use the courts to accomplish that goal.

Another barbaric practice returned to fashion is chain gangs, yet not without challenge. The *L.A. Times* on June 21, 1996, carried this excerpt:

> A year after becoming the first state to bring back chain gangs, Alabama has yielded to pressure and

permanently banned the practice... The shackling of five inmates together with leg irons as they work on roadside cleanup will be banned in Alabama under an agreement reached by lawyers for inmates, state prison officials, and Gov. Forrest "Fob" James Jr.

The settlement makes permanent a May 21 Corrections Department decision to quit chaining inmates together. That move was prompted by security problems: A guard fatally shot an inmate who attacked a fellow chain-gang member after being unchained to get back on the prison bus... After Alabama revived the chain gangs last year, Florida, Arizona, Wisconsin and Iowa all adopted forms of the work crews.

The *Times* carried a similar account in September 1996 in which "America's toughest sheriff," Phoenix's Joe Arpaio, proudly shackled 15 women together at the ankles in groups of five and put them to work cleaning the city's downtown streets. The prisoner-rights group **Middle Ground** protested on the cleanup route, labeling the ploy "a circus."

Chapter 12 – THE DRUG WAR AND INCARCERATION

John L. Mitchell and Sam Fullwood III collaborated on an article entitled "History Fuels Outrage Over Crack Allegations" for the *L.A. Times* October 22, 1996. The series in which the material appeared immediately drew criticism from various researchers as a sham piece of journalism, perhaps inspired by a coziness between the press and the intelligence community that stood accused of treasonous drug alliances. The following is from one of the stories within the story:

A VULNERABILITY TO CONSPIRACY THEORIES?

Black communities – freighted with a history of oppression, reeling from high rates of poverty and facing unprecedented cutbacks in federal social programs – are particularly vulnerable to conspiracy theories, scholars say.

The widespread acceptance of the allegation that the government helped steer crack to South-Central Los Angeles "says something about the isolation and lack of inclusion that African Americans experience in this society," said Florence Bonner, chairwoman of the sociology department at Howard University in Washington, D.C. "There is a feeling of isolation and disassociation from those very institutions that are there to support and involve us."

It becomes apparent when reading the collection of articles from the 3-part series in the *Times* that the editors have little worry about insulting the *good graces* of independent-thinking and well-read *Times* subscribers. The article tries to blame the *assumed paranoia* of the "Black community" for promulgating such grandiose plots as "Notions about an all-embracing conspiracy on the part of Jesuits or Freemasons, international capitalists, international Jews or communists..." – nonsense!

Despite such insults, the article goes on to note a credible history of anti-Black actions by government agencies to include: the U.S. Department of Health's notorious Tuskegee Syphilis Study, widespread Jim Crow statutes, government-sponsored human experimentation, the FBI's illegal COINTELPRO program, the leniency allowed the Korean murderer of a young girl named Latasha Harlins, the televised lynching of Rodney King and an uninterrupted history of racist police abuse, several highly publicized murders committed by whites but blamed on non-existent black predators, the disproportionate numbers of Blacks diagnosed with AIDS, targeting black elected officials for sting operations, disparities in debilitation from drugs and disease, and the great injustice of the enslavement of Africans by Europeans.

Any student of history can easily confirm that there are mounds of credible data to back up these specific racist episodes. It must be noted that the list mentioned above is but a fraction of *provable* misbehavior on the part of government agencies toward Native Americans, Blacks, Hispanics along with poor Whites, recent immigrants, and other undesirable social groups. This history includes accounts of sabotage of the Black community using drugs, alcohol and weapons which date as far back as the relationship between the WWII-era spy agency the U.S. Office of Strategic Services (OSS) and Sicilian-Mafia partisans which traded support for the invasion of Italy for the tacit approval for mobsters like Lucky Luciano to import heroin into Harlem.

Addressing the impact of drugs on the alarming rise in prison enrollment is an immense task. It is so overwhelming that mere recital of statistics only produces a sterile, impersonal perspective. The following is extracted from a broad source of highly credible, recently published sources:

- The *L.A. Times* noted in October 1996 that narcotics arrests for Los Angeles County rose from an annual total of 13, 453 in 1983 to 54, 497 in 1989, a four-fold increase blamed mainly on "widespread sale and use of crack cocaine, law enforcement and court officials say";

- According to a June 1996 GAO report entitled "Cocaine Treatment: Early Results from Various Approaches" (GAO/HEHS-96-80), in 1993 cocaine was linked to nearly 4,000 deaths, and cocaine admissions to state-supported drug programs increased from 39,000 people in 1985 to a shocking 200,000 in 1990 – more than a four-fold increase in a mere five years. An estimated $10 billion per year is lost in cocaine-related crimes and loss of productivity in addition to $1 billion per year in public and private treatment expenditures;

- The disparity between sentencing for crack cocaine offenses compared to powder cocaine is significant. A study published by the group **Families Against Discriminative Crack Law** in 1995 traces the sentences of 18 individuals who were convicted of crack cocaine violations that averaged 34 years. Yet had those same sentences been meted out under powder cocaine guidelines the average would have been three years *with* the possibility of parole;

- During the 12 years from 1980 to 1992, the Justice Department reported that the proportion of drug arrests resulting in imprisonment increased from 19 per 1,000 to 104 per 1,000, a rate 547% higher. In 1994, 60% of federal prisoners were being jailed for drug charges. (L.A. Times, October 28, 1994);

- The number of federal drug prosecutions increased from 8,775 in 1981 to 19,038 in 1988, according to an October 1996 study published by researchers from Syracuse University. During George Bush's first year as president, prosecutions increased nearly 27% over the previous year and saw a record number posted at the end of the Bush administration. Under Clinton, figures for drug prosecution fell for two years then rose again in 1995. The average number of drug prosecutions remained constant over the Bush and Clinton administrations;

- In February 1996, the 9th U.S. Circuit Court of Appeals ruled that the conviction of three Rastafarian residents of Montana should be overturned based because the trial judge "improperly barred evidence of their religious views." For many Rastas, the use of cannabis in religious ceremonies is fundamental to the practice of their religion. It is so illustrated in the Christian bible, which many but not all Rastas hold dear, according to Genesis 1:12 and Psalms 104. Thus the use of such religious sacrament is consistent with the federal 1993 Religious Freedom Restoration Act. This law was passed to correct a 1990 Supreme Court ruling letting stand the prosecution of Native Americans for the use of peyote, a longtime component of their religious ceremonies. The 1993 law requires a "compelling justification for any prosecution that substantially burdens a defendant's exercise of religion. A lawyer with the D.C.-based **Common Sense for Drug Policy** stated, "This is a legitimate religious issue for Rastafarians. They can't reach an appropriate religious state without ganja. It's like taking the wine out of the Catholic church." According to an *Associated Press* wire news account, the court ruled that "Rastafarianism, which originated in Jamaica, considers marijuana to be a religious sacrament that brings believers closer to divinity and enhances their spiritual unity." This ruling could have a significant impact on the status of thousands of prisoners throughout the nation convicted for possession or cultivation of cannabis;

- The *L.A. Times* reported September 13, 1994, that state prosecution of drug charges grew from 7% of inmates in 1983 to 25% in 1993, a nearly four-fold increase. From 1986 to 1991 prison rolls increased 51% yet violent crime rose only 15%, the vast differential can be attributed to the impact of drug convictions;

- Studies have demonstrated that 85% of criminal prosecutions against drug mothers have been of non-white women in the U.S. One doctor wrote in the book **SUBSTANCE AND SHADOW,** Harvard University Press, 1996, that "It seems politically safe to go after this population";

- The question of whether to continue treating drug users as a criminal or a health problem is increasingly raised due to the failure of the so-called "drug war" and the numbers of non-violent drug offenders clogging up the criminal justice system. On November 5, 1996 (a week from this writing), voters in Arizona were presented with

Proposition 200, which would mandate rehabilitation instead of jail for first and second-time nonviolent drug convicts. Proponents point to provisions which would steer users into drug treatment and education programs. According to syndicated columnist William Rasberry writing in the *L.A. Times*, November 1996, they point out the fact that "Much of the harmful effect of illegal drugs – at least the societal effect – stems less from the pharmacological damage done by the drugs than by the efforts at prohibition." These problems include "criminality, corruption of law enforcement, turf wars and 'executions'" Reactionary opponents of the measure, including the administration's new "drug czar" General Barry McCaffrey, have been firmly against the proposition. McCaffrey said, in the article, that the measure "is a cruel hoax wrapped up in some attractive ideas. It is going to be a disaster. It violates federal law, and it sends the wrong message to young people." Arizona has already voted in some of the country's most lenient rules for possession and cultivation of cannabis.

The following tables should be illustrative of the predominance of drug convictions on the tremendous increase in prison commitments. The statistics are from a June 1996 report from the U.S. DOJ Bureau of Justice Statistics, entitled "Correctional Populations in the United States, 1994" (NCJ-160091):

- Estimated number and percentage of prisoners in custody of State correctional authorities, by the most serious offense, 1980, 1985, 1990-94 – U.S. DOJ Bureau of Justice Statistics, 1994

Year	1980	1985	1990	1991	1992	1993	1994
Drug Offenses	19,000	38,900	148,600	155,200	172,300	183,200	202,100
	6.4%	8.6%	21.7%	21.3%	22.1%	22.1%	22.3%
Violent Offenses	173,300	246,200	313,600	339,500	370,300	395,700	429,400
	58.6%	54.5%	45.8%	46.6%	47.6%	047.8%	47.4%
Property Offenses	89,300	140,100	173,700	180,700	182,400	191,600	209,800
	30.2%	31.0%	25.4%	24.8%	23.4%	23.1%	23.2%
Total Jailed	295,819	451,812	684,544	728,495	778,495	828,566	906,112

- Number and percentage of prisoners in Federal prisons, by the most serious offense, 1980, 1985, 1990-94 – U.S. DOJ Bureau of Justice Statistics, 1994

Year	1980	1985	1990	1991	1992	1993	1994
Drug Offenses	4,900	9,482	30,470	36,782	42,879	48,997	51,823
	25.2%	34.3%	53.5%	55.9%	58.9%	59.2%	59.2%
Violent Offenses	6,572	7,768	9,557	9,852	9,506	11,058	11,429
	33.8%	28.1%	16.8%	15.0%	13.0%	13.4%	13.1%
Property Offenses	4,651	5,289	7,935	8,518	8,617	8,718	8,482
	23.9%	19.2%	13.9%	12.9%	11.8%	10.5%	9.7%
Total Jailed	19,471	27,607	56,989	65,802	72,851	82,698	87,515

Without a doubt, this country's "war on drugs" is inconsistent, paradoxical, and self-defeating. The U.S. allows legal drugs such as alcohol, nicotine, prescription, and over-the-counter medications to be abused on a vast level, promoted through billions of dollars of advertising each year. At the same time, America treats people who are addicted or are otherwise in the illicit drug trade as monsters. This hypocrisy will likely never of itself produce any long-term resolution to America's mushrooming drug and corrections problems.

Chapter 13 – DARK ALLIANCE: CIA-COCAINE SMUGGLING

An explosive series of articles written by researcher Gary Webb was published in August 1996 in the San Jose Mercury News, entitled "Dark Alliance: The Story Behind the Crack Explosion." Webb's series presents credible documentation that implicates U.S. intelligence involvement in a significant proportion of the dope smuggling that has contributed significantly to the rapid rise in imprisonment.

Webb's research is not the first to link Central Intelligence Agency managers of the anti-government Nicaraguan insurgency known as the *Contra War* to a slimy network of drug smugglers which arose to support the contras and generate mercenary profits in the meantime. The series has been instrumental in fueling a national outrage within the black community, which has been disproportionately injured by the widespread availability of cocaine, particularly crack.

Three principle charges have emerged from Webb's published articles: 1) a CIA-linked drug ring funneled portions of profits from domestic drug smuggling to the U.S.-backed Contra force; 2) this operation was instrumental in fueling the explosion of crack addiction in Los Angeles County; and 3) CIA, Drug Enforcement Agency and National Security Council officials frequently either turned a blind eye to the trafficking, tacitly approved of this method for funding covert military activities or covered up evidence of criminal activities. The same alliance between smugglers and the CIA is also attributed as the source of automatic firearms that came into the possession of L.A. drug dealers.

In September 1996, CIA Director John M. Deutch downplayed the charges stating that he'd found no evidence that the agency participated in *introducing crack cocaine* to the United States. Carefully examining the Director's words, one might note that his use of semantics might disguise existing "evidence" that the agency could be linked not to the introduction of *crack cocaine* but to the *cocaine used to manufacture crack,* which is one of the main charges made in the *San Jose Mercury News* series. Perhaps the director insults *our* intelligence with his reliance on such semantic tricks which an effective media should've easily seen through.

The origins of such a relationship between the national security establishment, including the military as well as intelligence and criminal drug enterprises smuggling into targeted neighborhoods, go back to the days preceding the Allied invasion of Italy during WWII. In planning to invade Italy through the island of Sicily, the Office of Strategic Services (OSS), the precursor to the CIA, cut a deal with the Sicily-based La Cosa Nostra. This dark alliance gave a virtual license for the mobster Lucky Luciano to import heroin into Harlem, New York, in quantities sufficient to sap the vitality out of the once-proud Black Mecca.

Later charges, back by mounds of yet-emerging testament, claimed that U.S. military officials were behind a scheme to distribute heroin obtained from southeast Asian "druglords" such as Thailand's notorious General Khun Sa, once said to be the leading figure for distribution of opium from the region's famous Golden Triangle. Occurring during the height of the Vietnam debacle, it was alleged that significant amounts of heroin were smuggled onto U.S. military facilities in the body cavities of war dead – identified by the so-called "red-tagging" of altered corpses.

Other credible reports have surfaced over the years of CIA and DEA cooperation with drug smugglers throughout Central and South America, Lebanon, Afghanistan, Pakistan, Haiti, and East Africa. Revelations emerged from Iran-Contra investigations linking the NSC with the likes of Col. Oliver North, Admiral John Poindexter, other military officers and private U.S. citizens involved with drug-dealing foreign officials, money launders, smugglers, arms dealers as well as other nations' intelligence agencies, such as the Israeli Mossad. All of them have been implicated in clandestine activities using drugs as a base of involvement.

Thus, those of us familiar with this unsavory history can regard the San Jose Mercury News articles' allegations not only as plausible but consistent with the nature of the U.S. agencies so implicated. This is also consistent with the record of oppressive governments throughout history who have used wholesale drug merchandising as a profitable enterprise. Such governments entities also use drugs for exerting behavior-modifying policies over vulnerable communities.

Chapter 14 – THE U.S. EXECUTION PROTOCOL

A disturbing fact, reported in the Long Beach Press-Telegram, September 6, 1994, in an article written by Bob Egelko, is that, as of July 1, 1994, *every one* of the 388 men and women on death row in California was too poor to afford to pay for a lawyer. This confirms the widely-held belief that judicial leniency in America is reserved for those who have the cash to buy-in. In reality, there was, at that time, not a single wealthy person to be found among the 2800 prisoners on death row in the U.S.

Across America, states race to bring the condemned to their final date with the executioner. President Clinton's home state of Arkansas, on August 3, 1994, conducted the nation's first triple execution in 32 years. This century's record for the number of prisoners sent by any given state to the execution chamber was Virginia, who electrocuted eight men on February 1-2, 1951. The nation's one-day record for executions was the hanging of 38 Dakota Indians by federal officials in 1862 after the tribe declared war on the United States for failing to honor treaties.

Since the U.S. Supreme Court overturned the ban on the death penalty in 1976, Texas has led the nation with 76 executions through May 1994. Of the then-2800 prisoners on death row, 1.5% were female. Since 1985, nine persons under age 18 have been executed. The United States is one of only seven countries that permit the execution of children.

Today the preferred method of execution is lethal injection. In 1995, California was temporarily barred from using the gas chamber because it had been challenged in federal court as an inhumane form of execution that violated constitutional protections against "cruel and unusual punishment." Without hesitation, California joined 24 others, of the 39 states which allow execution with the use of lethal injection.

The 1994 Clinton Crime Control Act authorized 60 federal crimes, 50 of which were new, which are punishable by death ranging from the murder of government officials to espionage to being a "drug kingpin." Ironically, the new law imposes the death penalty for such crimes as the murder of a U.S. national abroad, willful deprivation of federal rights resulting in death, use of weapons of mass destruction resulting in death as well as genocide.

The following table of statistics highlights the imposition of the death penalty in America. The figures are from the Department of Justice:

- Summary characteristics of all prisoners present at yeard end received from the court, or removed from death row, 1994 – DOJ Correctional Populations in the United States, 1996

Demographic Group	On death row at yearend 1994	Received from a court in 1994	Sentence Executed	Removed by means other than execution
U.S. Total	2,890	306	31	112
Male	2,849	301	31	112
Female	41	5	0	0
White	1,645	162	20	72
Black	1,197	136	11	39
Hispanic (includes	224	25	1	9

Evidence is widespread of the discriminatory imposition of the death penalty as well as to its failure as a deterrent in overall crime trends. According to a report from the **Death Penalty Information Center**, between 1970 and 1994, 48 people were removed from death row because of evidence of their innocence has surfaced. New York Times columnist Anna Quindlen in November 1994 cited the tremendous cost of the lengthy court process of motions, appeals, and hearings. Her column gives examples of states such as Florida, which spent $60 million over 15 years to execute 18 persons, and Texas, where each death penalty prosecution averages some $2 million -- three times the cost of high-security containment for life.

Chapter 15 – SOCIAL TRENDS INTENSIFIED THE CRISIS

There are a large number of social, political, and economic factors that have contributed to the massive surge in prison populations in the United States. Numerous studies exist, and new ones are produced continuously, that follow individual trends like poverty, poor education, the influence of electronic media and racism.   Such studies closely scrutinize various social issues for their impact on the criminal justice system.

While under the scope of this analysis, it is difficult to be comprehensive on the impact of poverty, unemployment, racism, inflation, the media and entertainment, failed education, biology, and the social environment on the system. I can attempt to point out a few areas which have demonstrated a significant influence on the rapid swell in numbers of incarcerated in the U.S.

- A study, published by the **Center on Juvenile and Criminal Justice**, traced the shift of spending priorities for the state of California and published some rather shocking findings in late October 1996.   When comparing state spending for prisons to funding for higher education, using the periods from 1980-81 and 1996-97 as bases for comparison, the remarkable shift in priority from education toward incarceration becomes apparent.   During the earlier period, California spent 8.2% of its general fund for higher education, while 2.3% went to corrections. But 16 years later that more than three to one ratio had disappeared, and the current budget for prisons is a whopping 9.4% while higher education gets 8.7%.   The devastating effect of such budget priorities and the crises involving detention, economics, and education for Black students were among the main themes of a report, entitled **"From Class Rooms to Cell Blocks: The Effects of Prison Building on Higher Education and African American Enrollment."** The report revealed that the ratio of Black men in prison to those enrolled in higher education was 4 to 1 – and the increase of prison enrollment, for young Black men, between 1980 and 1995 was nearly *20 times greater than* increased participation in institutions of higher learning.

- Researcher Harris L. Coulter points out the role of *vaccinations* in the causation of widespread developmental disabilities, a fact which cannot be underappreciated. He also points out that despite a predominance of poor in the so-called criminal class, "sociopathic crime is rather evenly distributed across the American class structure." He wrote of the probable role of vaccines in contributing to likely biological origins of much of this antisocial behavior in a landmark 1990 book, ***VACCINATION, SOCIAL VIOLENCE AND CRIMINALITY: THE MEDICAL ASSAULT ON THE AMERICAN BRAIN***:

"[D]evelopmental disabilities" are nearly always generated by encephalitis. And the primary cause of encephalitis in the United States and other industrialized countries is the childhood vaccination program.

To be specific, a large proportion of the millions of U.S. children and adults suffering from autism, seizures, mental retardation, hyperactivity, dyslexia, and other shoots and branches of the hydra-headed entity called "developmental disabilities," owe their disorders to one or another of the vaccines against childhood diseases.

The so-called "sociopathic personality," which is at the root of the enormous increase in crime of the past two decades, is also largely rooted in vaccine damage.

...Every day this program continues, hundreds of normal healthy babies are turned into defective goods: mentally retarded, blind, deaf, autistic, epileptic, learning-disabled, emotionally unstable, future juvenile delinquents, and career criminals.

...The problems of black youth are, of course, notorious. In all educational categories they perform worse than whites, and society's production of an uneducated, seemingly uneducable mass of blacks generates much of the crime and drug-abuse which today disfigure the social landscape. Is there a possibility that blacks could be disfavored even more than whites by the vaccination programs?

Admittingly, there is a shortage of research that has been conducted on the specifics of the impact of vaccination on violent behaviors. But what data has been examined suggests that these injections have an even more destructive effect on the neurolgic status of Blacks.

...Blacks are also known to suffer more than whites from conditions which are recognizably the sequelae of encephalitis, such as epilepsy and asthma. The incidence of asthma in American black children is two and a half times what it is in whites; and the death rate from asthma is three times higher.

- Under provisions of the new federal welfare law, California, the state which is the nation's largest care provider for undocumented immigrants, plans to mail notices to 70,000 pregnant women statewide, which will eliminate state funding of prenatal care on December 1, 1996. This plan can be expected to be accompanied by increased risks of birth complications, emergency room costs, and unanticipated additional costs in the long term – adding to the broad social malaise which unfits so many for full participation as contributors to society.

- Reversing a downward trend in the late 1980s, drug consumption by students in the U.S. began rising dramatically in the 1990s. A state report published in August 1996 found drug use in 6 categories (alcohol, marijuana, amphetamine, LSD, heroin, and cocaine) rising among nearly 6,000 students surveyed from November 1995 to March 1996. A newly-released federal study found drug use among 12 to 17-year olds rose from 5.3% of those surveyed in 1992 to 10.9% in 1995 – *an increase of 105% in a mere three years.*

- "In 1993 prescription drugs generated illicit market sales of $25 billion (the figure for cocaine and crack was $31 billion) – so said an *L.A. Times* editorial decrying the failure of the so-called "drug war" to address the issue of widespread abuse of prescription drugs. The article also noted that legal drugs are responsible for about half the drug-related emergency room admissions in recent years. Too often, those responsible for such trafficking are allowed to escape prosecution, such as physicians who over-prescribe drugs, along with other individuals who illegally cop pharmaceutical prescriptions for the rich, the famous, and the well-connected. The August 1996 *Times* editorial also cited an incidence where "federal officers arrested a drug runner carrying at least $600,000 worth of Dilaudid, a heroin-like drug. Rather than prosecuting him, the agents utilized him as an informant in a small-potatoes cocaine case. He eventually went free." Widespread self-medication is another under-reported drug problem with sales of over-the-counter drugs racking up $16.1 billion in sales in 1995.

- The wealth gap between the haves and the have-nots in America is appalling. An October report from the group **Bread for the World** cited statistics that: 21.5% of U.S. minors live in poverty, a ratio far above other developed countries; the next-highest industrialized country, Australia, has 14.1% of its children in poverty; Finland, which had the lowest rate among developed nations, had 2.5% of its children impoverished. Second only to Russia, the U.S. also had the highest gap between the incomes of rich and poor. According to the study, "one out of four American children is habitually hungry or in danger of hunger."

- The impact of electronic media — movies, television, radio, and electronic games — in popularizing a culture of lawlessness cannot be underappreciated. Certain groups do issue reports like the one published by the **UCLA Center for Communication Policy** in October 1996, which argues that networks have made significant progress toward reducing gratuitous violence, sex, drugs, and moral decay in their media. A cursory analysis of current programming shows that things haven't changed much: titillation used to make up for lack of creativity;

more catastrophes, explosions, and gunshots than can be counted in any single week of broadcast; a pervasive culture of sex, drugs, and violence in pop video culture; monsters and demons to fuel the nightmares of young minds; video gore and electronic "nuke-em-up" proceeding unchecked – I think we see the pattern here. Expecting the entertainment industry to improve its creative content is like asking a porcupine to shed its quills – it won't happen soon!

- A national random telephone survey sponsored jointly by **The Washington Post,** the **Kaiser Family Foundation**, and **Harvard University**, conducted in the fall of 1995, determined that most white Americans have "fundamental misconceptions" about the economic and social circumstances of African-Americans. Numerous race-based misperceptions were mentioned in the lengthy survey including divergent opinions on whether Blacks have or have not achieved equality concerning civil rights; whether racism and discrimination is a big problem in America today; have Blacks had an equal chance to succeed; how much responsibility do Whites bear, if any, for the issues which affect Blacks; and the role of the federal government in guaranteeing equal access to jobs, equitable pay, and housing. Both black and white agreed that the federal government did have a role to play to assure fair treatment by the courts and police. Both share a pessimism over the near future in America. Comparisons between rich and poor Whites yielded similar contrasts in perceptions about social problems, suggesting that the difference between overall black and white impressions stems in no small part from economic or class differentials. *The Washington Post* profiled the survey in an October 1995 article by Richard Morin, which read in part:

A majority of white Americans have fundamental misconceptions about the economic circumstances of black Americans, according to a new national survey, with most saying that the average black is faring as well or better than the average white in such specific areas as jobs, education and health care.

That's not true. Government statistics show that whites, on average, earn 60 percent more than blacks, are far more likely to have medical insurance and more than twice as likely to graduate from college.

Most of those surveyed, regardless of race, also greatly overestimated the number of minority Americans in the United States. Most whites, blacks, Hispanics and Asian Americans said the black population, which is about 12 percent, was twice that size. Those whites with the most inaccurate ideas about the size of the minority populations were the most likely to say that further increases would be bad for the country.

"There is real meaning, substantive meaning in these numbers," said Richard Neimi, a political scientist at the University of Rochester who has studied the relationship between knowledge and attitudes. "People do misunderstand what the country is like. They overestimate... And it is not a big leap to imagine that this may well affect the way people think about minorities, that it may lead to this idea that the country is being overrun."

The article further corrected some of these misperceptions, using statistics extracted from U.S. census figures, in a couple of paragraphs labeled "Reality Check":

> In 1994, 28.6 percent of whites held professional or managerial jobs, as compared to 18.7 percent of blacks. In contrast, 22.5 percent of blacks worked in low-end service jobs compared to 12.6 percent of whites... Young whites still are more than twice as likely to finish college and are less likely to drop out of high school... In 1990, the average value of homes owned by whites was $80,300. For blacks, that figure was $50,500. Whites are nearly twice as likely to be homeowners as blacks.

> In 1990, the average white family earned $37,630, while the average black family earned $22,470. SOURCES: Washington Post/Kaiser Family Foundation/Harvard University survey, Bureau of Labor Statistics, 1990 census.

- Racial scapegoating has emerged as an issue affecting young Blacks, as illustrated by two high-profile cases in which white murderers nearly successfully pinned their crimes on nonexistent black suspects. In Union, South Carolina, Susan Smith garnered the attention of the national news media as she tearfully pleaded for days that a nonexistent black carjacker return her two infant children. Only after law officials began to doubt her story did the truth emerge that she had strapped her babies into their car seats and sent them to their death in the depths of a local lake.

  In 1989 a white Boston businessman, Charles Stuart, had used a similar ploy to cover up the murder of his pregnant wife, whom he had killed for her life insurance.

For three weeks after Stuart's accusation that a mythical black man had killed his wife and shot Stuart himself, police in Massachusetts went on a spree terrorizing the black population of Boston before Stuart, the real murderer, killed himself in January 1990. Another renowned case, was that of Jesse Anderson, killed in a Wisconsin prison along with the cannibal Jeffrey Dahmer. Anderson had falsely accused two black men of murdering his wife. Anderson and Dahmer were beaten to death by a fellow black inmate, Cristopher J. Scarver, whom many Africans consider to be a folk hero.

Chapter 16 – JAILED YOUTH: A STOLEN FUTURE

It is a well-established fact that the level of civility of a nation is based upon how they display compassion and nurturing toward youth. By extension, a similar degree of civility will be shown in those youth as they mature into productive and responsible citizens. As the alarming statistics on the rapid growth in incarceration in the United States indicate, particularly affecting Black populations, we are in for a stormy future as we stand at the cusp of a new millennium. If the jailing trends continue as they have since 1980, this country will be turned into one big lockup – and large numbers of those under heavy security may not be the ones in jail.

Already whole neighborhoods are being turned into concentration camps. This occurs not only in the inner-city areas that are the arena for the vast majority of criminal activities but also for more affluent neighborhoods that are now building gated communities, spending increasing resources on electronic surveillance systems, private security networks, and growing ever-more apprehensive each year. Feeding this frenzy, the media huffs a hysterical breeze to fan the fires of xenophobia and paranoia further. Who is the ultimate victim in the insanity which American has engaged upon – the whole business of condemning so many to the criminal justice system?

The victims are varied and include those youth whose visions of happiness and productivity are clouded by the too-real risk of violence or criminal prosecution. What of the elderly, so often the easy prey of property crimes, who have to live their retirement behind high security and high suspicion? Women find themselves increasingly at risk of violence and sexual assault, and such attacks threaten wider and younger populations as years progress.

The enormous redirection of funds away from higher education and into prison construction gives us a clear indication where America is investing its future. Let us be clear that for the foreseeable future, no real change of direction can be expected from elected officials, government agencies, or corporate investors. This is exacerbated by the rising disparities between Black and White, rich and poor, urban and suburban. Add to the mix the persistence of high rate of unemployment (which oddly signal *good news* for financial investment markets), the persistent menace of racism, the "dumbing down" of public education, "Three Strikes" legislation, and most obvious, the complete and utter failure of the "war on drugs." The writing on the wall is clear – the U.S. is headed for the dumps.

The issue of political prisoners is something for which the U.S. has hypocritically castigated nations such as China, Nigeria, and other developing countries. America remains reluctant to judge itself by a similar standard. Jailed political activists like Geronimo ji Jaga Pratt, Mumia Abu Jamaal, Leonard Peltier, Yahweh ben Yahweh, Sundiata Acoli, Alejandrina Torres, Alberto Rodriguez, and many dozens more stand in the face of America as a reminder of the seedy undercurrent of political injustice and hypocrisy which remains pervasive in the 1990s.

The single case of Geronimo Pratt, who has languished in prison for 25 years, over eight of which in isolation, for a murder which the FBI had always possessed direct evidence of his innocence. The injustice of Pratt's case alone reveals this nation in a moral and ethical morass of which it cannot extract itself. Yet for every high profile political prisoner such as Pratt, Leonard Peltier, Yahweh ben Yahweh or Mumia Abu Jamaal, whose cases are kept in the public eye by dedicated groups, there are a dozen more political prisoners languishing in confinement throughout the country, ignored by the media and largely overlooked by those who they stood up for in the first place.

And what of a future where there are record numbers of the so-called "Baby Boomers" in retirement? Where is the large workforce which will be required to produce a surplus to sustain such a considerable body of retirees? Who will pay for the expected explosion of senior citizens? Is it possible, or even likely, that efforts to re-legitimize euthanasia (killing of the old, the invalid, and the mentally defective) such as the high-profile saga of "suicide doctor" Jack Kevorkian are indicative of a growing social trend toward killing excess population? Might this proceed so far as to possibly fulfill macabre prophecies of 60s-era fright films such as *Soylent Green* and *The Andromeda Strain*, deliberate policies to kill off excess population and to even use their corpses for food or fertilizer?

The strength of a nation ultimately lies in the ability of its 18 to 50-year-old workforce to produce a surplus. That task becomes *impossible* if as many as 30 to 50 percent of that workforce is incarcerated, chronically underemployed, substance-addicted, or otherwise unproductive. The outlook for Blacks in America appears bleak when we are considered as a single, widely-dispersed community. As an African-centered researcher, I conclude that the harsh outlook for my community in the foreseeable future is too great for me just to live as comfortable as I can, merely watching out for my own narrow interests.

Yet, a researcher is burdened with the time and concentration it takes to produce quality studies. Without the assistance of community leaders, elected officials, the media, financial investors, and managers who can guide the masses toward specific, pre-planned actions — I experience frustration due to the very quality of the research and over the projections that research generates. I recently strayed from the detached arena as a journalist researcher to actively challenge a particularly offensive act. Several government agencies and the Kaiser Foundation were exposed for having injected *over a thousand black and brown babies* in a horrible L.A. County measles vaccine experiment. After three months of passionate commitment, thousands of dollars invested, and hundreds of hours of pleading for the people to *do something* about this crime, I became bitter and frustrated over the lack of interest in the broader community. There is only so much that one can do for someone else. At a point, people are going to have to stand up and do for themselves. The only option, at this point in history, may be the choice between self-reliance or death!

The future for Blacks in the United States is severely limited due in no small part to current trends in law enforcement, the criminal justice system, and the boom in prisons. Until the jailing trends illustrated in this report are measurably reversed, and the tattered social fabric is mended, we can expect only further pressure from agencies linked to the crisis. I believe that the trend toward incarceration can ultimately be reversed, and I trust that this report will somehow contribute to that recovery.

BIBLIOGRAPHY FOR THIS SPECIAL REPORT

1) AN AMERICAN DILEMMA: THE NEGRO PROBLEM AND MODERN DEMOCRACY by Gunnar Myrdal, Harper & Row, New York, Twentieth Anniversary edition, 1962

2) CORRECTIONAL POPULATIONS IN THE UNITED STATES, 1994 from the Bureau of Justice Statistics, U.S. Dept. of Justice, NCJ-160091, June 1996

3) NUMBERS OF INMATES HITS RECORD HIGH from Associated Press, printed in the Long Beach Press Telegram, June 2, 1994

4) MAIN STREET FINDS GOLD IN URBAN CRIME WAVE by David Lamb, L.A. Times, October 9, 1996

5) THEY'RE SOLD ON SOFT CELL APPROACH: INMATES PAY TO STAY AT SMALL JAILS by Solomon Moore, L.A. Times, October 20, 1996

6) PRISONS: CALIFORNIA'S GROWTH INDUSTRY by John Jacobs, Long Beach Press Telegram, August 12, 1994

7) BLOCK UNVEILS PROPOSAL TO OPEN TWIN TOWERS JAIL by Josh Meyer and Jeffrey L. Rabin, L.A. Times, September 13, 1996

8) QUESTIONS WHIRL AROUND SHERIFF BLOCK'S NUMBERS, editorial in the L.A. Times, September 16, 1996

9) GO WEST, YOUNG MAN, AND GROW UP WITH THE PRISONS by Russell Baker, Long Beach Press Telegram, February 2, 1994

10) CALIFORNIA'S PROFUSION OF PRISONS by Dan Morain, L.A. Times, October 16, 1994

11) CALIFORNIA SHORT ON CELLS FOR BAD GUYS by Mark Katches, Los Angeles Daily News correspondent, printed in the Long Beach Press Telegram, January 1, 1994

12) CRIME: PRISON PROPOSAL, ECONOMICS AND THE IMAGE PROBLEM by Willard H. Murray Jr., Assemblyman, 52nd District, L.A. Times, September 29, 1994

13) END THE FISCAL ABSURDITY OF ADDING PRISONS by Tom Hennessy, Long Beach Press Telegram, October 16, 1994

14) GOVERNOR SIGNS BILL BARRING STATE FROM BUYING FOREIGN GOODS MADE BY SLAVE LABOR by Stuart Silverstein, L.A. Times, October 1, 1996

15) CALIFORNIA GUARDS KILL MORE INMATES THAN NATION'S 7 MAJOR PRISON SYSTEMS, Associated Press Wire Service, Long Beach Press Telegram, September 1, 1994

16) MAIL CORRESPONDENCE from Jeffrey M. Hill (4-B), Reg. No. 40971-133, PO Box 2000, Allenwood F.C.I. (Med.), White Deer, PA 17887-2000

17) DARK ALLIANCE: AMERICA'S CRACK PLAGUE'S HAS ROOTS IN NICARAGUAN WAR; SHADOWY ORIGINS OF 'CRACK' EPIDEMIC and WAR ON DRUGS HAS UNEQUAL IMPACT ON BLACK AMERICANS, by Gary Webb, San Jose Mercury News, August 18-20, 1996

18) EXAMINING CHARGES OF CIA ROLE IN CRACK SALES written by John McManus, L.A. Times, October 21, 1996

19) HISTORY FUELS OUTRAGE OVER CRACK ALLEGATIONS by John L. Mitchell and Sam Fulwood III, L.A. Times, October 22, 1996

20) CIA SEEKS MORE TIME FOR DRUG INQUIRY by David Willman, L.A. Times, October 24, 1996

21) HUMAN GUINEA PIGS by Harriet A. Washington, Emerge, October 1994

22) IS MILITARY RESEARCH HAZARDOUS TO VETERANS' HEALTH? LESSONS SPANNING HALF A CENTURY, the Rockefeller Report, December 8, 1994, 103rd Congress, 2nd

Session U.S. Senate, S. Prt. 103-7, Chairman John D. Rockefeller IV

23) ADVISORY COMMITTEE ON ETHICS IN HUMAN EXPERIMENTATION: EXPERIMENTATION GUIDLINES created by C. Trueman, 1995 University of New England, Armidale, NSW, 2351, obtained from the Internet

24) VETERANS DISABILITY: INFORMATION FROM MILITARY MAY HELP VA ASSESS CLAIMS RELATED TO SECRET TESTS, GAO Report to the Chairman, Committee on Veterans' Affairs, U.S. Senate, February 1993, GAO/NSIAD 93-89

25) NO CONSENSUS ON CHEMICAL CASTRATION by Shari Roan, L.A. Times, September 26, 1996

26) BAD MEDICINE? - IS JOHNS HOPKINS' RESEARCH HELPING OR HURTING HAITI'S POOR? by Worth Cooley-Prost and John Canham-Clyne, Baltimore City Paper, September 4, 1996

27) Newsletter of FAMILIES AGAINST DISCRIMINATIVE CRACK LAW, published by the African Cultural Society, Milton X FADCL/President, January 28, 1995, PO Box 1000, Leavenworth, KS 66048-1000

28) NUMBERS BELIE TOUGHNESS ON CRIME by Vincent Schiraldi, L.A. Times, October 18, 1994

29) PUNISHING WITHOUT HELPING, letter to the editor written by Bruce Derrickson, Long Beach Press Telegram, April 13, 1994

30) STERNER PENALTIES SEND U.S. PRISONER COUNT PAST 1 MILLION by Elizabeth Shogren, L.A. Times, October 29, 1994

31) GUARDS' BULLETS GO ASTRAY by Marc Lifsher and Kim Christensen, Orange County Register, October 24, 1994

32) FBI INVESTIGATING DEATHS AT PRISON by Dan Morain and Daniel M. Weintraub, L.A. Times, October 27, 1994

33) GUARD SLAYINGS OF PRISONERS IN STATE ARE HIGH by Dan Morain and John Hurst, L.A. Times, October 17, 1994

34) SENATE VOTES TO REPEAL INMATE BILL OF RIGHTS by Carl Ingram, L.A. Times, April 8, 1994

35) SETTLEMENT WILL BAN ALABAMA'S PRISON CHAIN GANGS from Associated Press, printed in the L.A. Times, June 21, 1996

36) TOUGH SHERIFF PUTS WOMEN IN CHAIN GANG from Associated Press, printed in the L.A. Times, September 20, 1996

37) PUNISH OR PROTECT? by Lynn Smith, L.A. Times, September 3, 1996

38) DRUG-CASE RISE HAS LEVELED, STUDY SHOWS from Associated Press, printed in the L.A. Times, October 20, 1996

39) STIFF DRUG LAWS CITED FOR RECORD INCARCERATION RATE by David G. Savage, L.A. Times, September 13, 1994

40) COURT RULES ON RASTAFARIANS from Associated Press, February 2, 1996, accessed on the Internet

41) RED, GOLD AND GREEN DOLLARS: RASTAFARIANISM IN AMERICA TODAY by Alex Costa, Hot Lava Magazine, October 1996

42) COCAINE TREATMENT: EARLY RESULTS FROM VARIOUS APPROACHES from the U.S. General Accounting Office, Report to Congressional Requesters, June 1996 (GAO/HEHS-96-80)

43) Editorial appearing in the Long Beach Press Telegram by New York Times columnist Anna Quindlen, November 22, 1994

44) EXECUTIONS IN AMERICA, researched by D'Jamila Salem, L.A. Times, May 11, 1994

45) DO ONLY POOR PEOPLE LIVE ON DEATH ROW? by Bob Egelko, Associated Press, printed in the Long Beach Press Telegram, September 6, 1994

46) ARK. HOLDS NATION'S FIRST TRIPLE EXECUTION IN 32 YEARS from Associated Press, printed in the Long Beach Press Telegram, August 4, 1994

47) VACCINATION, SOCIAL VIOLENCE, AND CRIMINALITY: THE MEDICAL ASSAULT ON THE AMERICAN BRAIN by Harris L. Coulter, 1990, North Atlantic Books, PO Box 12327, Berkeley, CA 94701

48) WILSON SETS PRENATAL CARE CUTOFF DEC. 1 by Patrick J. McDonnell, L.A. Times, October 24, 1996

49) DRUG USE AMONG STUDENTS UP, STATE POLL FINDS from Associated Press, printed in the L.A. Times, August 27, 1996

50) WHEN IT COMES TO DRUGS, LEGAL DOESN'T MEAN SAFE an editorial in the L.A. Times, August 25, 1996

51) AMERICA'S OTHER DRUG PROBLEM by Linda Marsa, L.A. Times Magazine September 29, 1996

52) ARIZONA'S RADICAL IDEA: PAROLE DRUGGIES by William Rasbery, L.A. Times, November 1, 1996

53) U.S. CHILDHOOD POVERTY CITED AS HIGHEST OF RICH NATIONS' by Norman Kempster, L.A. Times, October 17, 1996

54) A DISTORTED IMAGE OF MINORITIES by Richard Morin, The Washington Post, October 8, 1995

55) PRISON SPENDING HURTS SCHOOLS AND BLACK STUDENTS, REPORT SAYS by Elaine Woo, L.A. Times, October 23, 1996

56) VIOLENCE ON NETWORK TV DECLINES, STUDY SAYS by Brian Lowry, L.A. Times, October 16, 1996

57) CAMP CRACKDOWN by Elizabeth Mehren, fourth installment of the series "Girl Trouble: America's Overlooked Crime Problem, L.A. Times June 19, 1996

58) PUNISH OR PROTECT? by Lynn Smith, L.A. Times, September 3, 1996

59) 80% OF JAILED WOMEN AWAITING TRIAL HAVE BEEN MENTALLY ILL, STUDY FINDS from the L.A. Times, June 20, 1996

60) REPORT ASSAILS NATION'S JUVENILE DETENTION FACILITIES from Associated Press, printed in the L.A. Times, September 26, 1994

61) YOUTH, CRIME AND PUBLIC MONEY, an editorial in the L.A. Times, June 25, 1996

62) GANGS by James C. Howell, Ph.D., obtained from the web site of the U.S. DOJ Office of Juvenile Justice and Delinquency Prevention, April 1994 <http://www.ncjrs.org/txtfiles/fs-9411.txt>

63) CAL STATE, YOUTH PRISON UNIT VIE FOR CAMARILLO HOSPITAL by Kenneth R. Weiss and Jeff McDonald, L.A. Times, September 16, 1996

64) EARLIER NURTURE FOR YOUNG MINDS, an editorial in the L.A. Times, October 16, 1996

65) VIOLENT CRIMES BY JUVENILES DOWN FIRST TIME IN 7 YEARS by Robert L. Jackson, L.A. Times, August 9, 1996

66) JUVENILE HALL IS ADDING WING FOR VIOLENT OFFENDERS by Jeannette Regalado, L.A. Times, August 21, 1994

67) A NATIONAL SURVEY OF AFTERCARE PROVISIONS FOR BOOT CAMP GRADUATES, from the U.S. Department of Justice, National Institute of Justice, May 1996

68) JUVENILE JUSTICE: DEINSTITUTIONALIZING STATUS OFFENDERS – A RECORD OF PROGRESS from the U.S. DOJ Office of Juvenile Justice and Delinquency Prevention, Fall/Winter 1995

69) DISPROPORTIONATE MINORITY REPRESENTATION by Mark Roscoe and Reggie Morton, obtained from the web site of

the U.S. DOJ Office of Juvenile Justice and Delinquency Prevention, April 1994 <http://www.ncjrs.org/txtfiles/fs-9411.txt>

70) WHAT'S LOST WITHIN THE SAFETY OF GATES by Bob Andrews, L.A. Times, October 17, 1996

71) 1 INMATE KILLED, 13 HURT IN PRISON FIGHT by Dan Morain, L.A. Times, September 28, 1996

72) IMPACT OF 3 STRIKES LESS THAN EXPECTED by Dan Morain, L.A. Times, October 25, 1996

73) THE AMERICAN WAY: BLAME A BLACK MAN by Lee A. Daniels, Emerge Magazine, February 1995

74) PRIVATE PRISONS: PROFITS OF CRIME by Phil Smith, CovertAction Quarterly No. 46, Fall 1993

75) WELFARE LAW'S JOB GOAL MAY BE IMPOSSIBLE by Carlos Rivera, L.A. Times November 4, 1996

INDEX

CUTTING EDGE RESEARCH TO SERVE AN EMERGING LEADERSHIP
PANIC
What the Coronavirus Pandemic Tells Us About the State of the World
Keidi Obi Awadu
Author of the Conscious Rasta Report

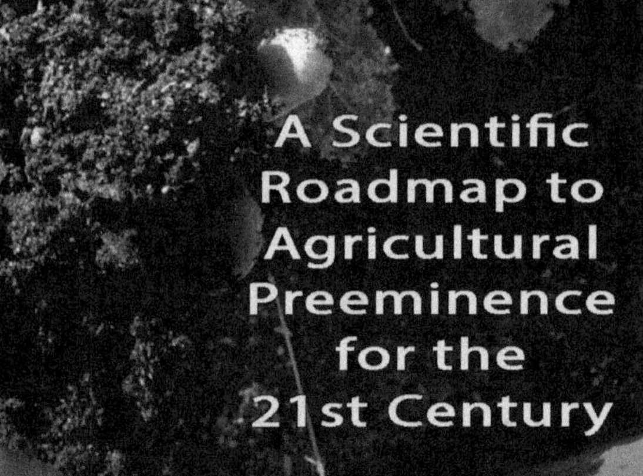
CUTTING-EDGE RESEARCH FOR AN EMERGING LEADERSHIP
THE
Blackest Soil
Africa Can Feed the World
A Scientific
Roadmap to
Agricultural
Preeminence
for the
21st Century
Keidi Obi Awadu
Author of the Conscious Rasta Report

Africa Rising
DAWN IS BREAKING OVER AFRICA
Keidi Obi Awadu
Author of the Conscious Rasta Report

thiopian
KENYA
KIPCHOGE
MADE IN AFRICA

Cutting Edge Research to Serve an Emerging Leadership
FUTURENOMIC$
Positioning Your
Enterprise to Win
in the New
Global Economy
Keidi Obi Awadu
Author of the Conscious Rasta Report

Cutting Edge Research to Serve an Emerging Leadership

The
REPAIRING

Making Reparations Practical

Keidi Obi Awadu

Author of the Conscious Rasta Report

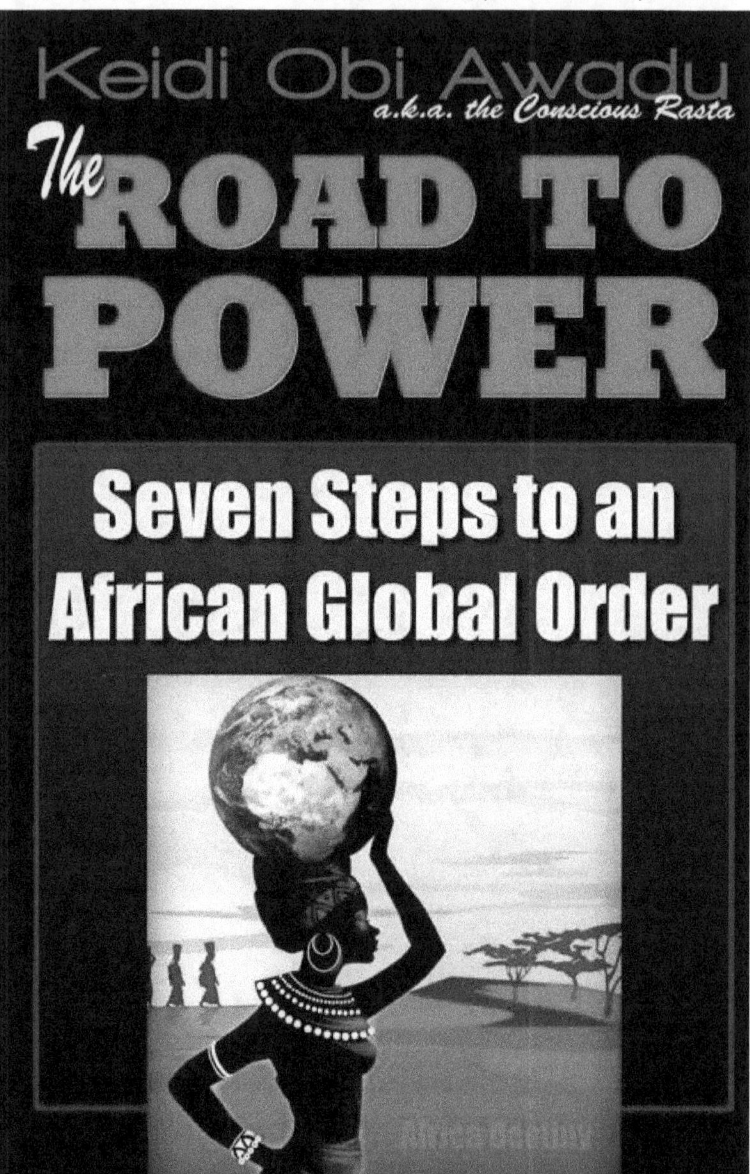
Keidi Obi Awadu
a.k.a. the Conscious Rasta
The ROAD TO POWER
Seven Steps to an
African Global Order